The Composers' Specials
TEACHER'S GUIDE
from The Devine Entertainment Video Series

Listening Guides, Discussion Topics and
Cross Curricular Activities

By Betsy Henderson

**Published by HAL LEONARD CORPORATION
and DEVINE ENTERTAINMENT
www.devinetime.com**

DEVINE ENTERTAINMENT
CORPORATION

DISTRIBUTED BY
HAL•LEONARD® CORPORATION
7777 W. BLUEMOUND RD. P.O. BOX 13819 MILWAUKEE, WI 53213

Copyright © 2000 by HAL LEONARD CORPORATION and DEVINE ENTERTAINMENT
International Copyright Secured   All Rights Reserved

This publication may not be reproduced in any form or by any means,
except where indicated, without the prior written permission of the Publisher.

TABLE OF CONTENTS

BACH'S FIGHT FOR FREEDOM
    Biographical Information.............................5
Fact Finding As You Watch......................6
Putting the Puzzle Together....................7
    Dissecting the Story..................................7
    Vocabulary..8
Filing the Facts Away..............................9
    Background Research...............................9
    Time Tunnel..10
    All in a Day's Work.................................10
    Instrumentally Speaking........................11
    Matching Wits..12
    Reaching for New Heights....................12
Stepping Across the Curriculum...........13
    Language Arts (Writing).........................13
    Theater Arts...13
    Social Studies..14
    Creative Arts..14
Student Activities #1, #2, #3............15-16
Listening to the Music of Bach..............17
    Overture No. 2 in B minor, Badinerie.......17
    Listening Map #1...................................18
    Overture No. 3 in D Major, II Air............19
    Listening Map #2...................................20

HANDEL'S LAST CHANCE
    Biographical Information.........................21
Fact Finding As You Watch....................22
Putting the Puzzle Together..................23
    "Handel" With Care................................23
    Vocabulary..24
Getting a "Handel" on Facts..................25
    Background Research.............................25
    Instrumentally Speaking........................27
    The Musical Language..........................29
    Can You "Handel" These?.....................29

Stepping Across the Curriculum...........30
    Language Arts (Writing).........................30
    Social Studies..30
    Creative Arts..31
    Musical Experiments.............................31
Student Activities #4, #5, #6............32-33
Listening to the Music of Handel..........34
    Hallelujah Chorus (from the MESSIAH)....34
    Listening Map #3...................................35
    Hornpipe, from the Water Music Suite......36
    Listening Map #4...................................37

ROSSINI'S GHOST
    Biographical Information.........................38
Fact Finding As You Watch....................39
Putting the Puzzle Together..................40
    The World of Opera...............................40
    Categories of Voices.............................40
    Vocabulary..41
Filing the Facts Away............................42
    Background Research.............................42
    Fill in the Blanks....................................43
    Unscramble These Words.....................43
    The Curse on the Barber of Seville Opera...44
    Reaching for New Heights....................45
Stepping Across the Curriculum...........46
    Language Arts (Writing).........................46
    Musical Experiments.............................46
    Theater Arts...47
Student Activities #7, #8.......................48
Listening to the Music of Rossini..........49
    Overture to Il Barbiere di Siviglia............49
    Listening Map #5...................................50
    Overture to Guillaume Tell.....................51
    Listening Map #6...................................52

LISZT'S RHAPSODY
 Biographical Information 53
Fact Finding As You Watch 54
Putting the Puzzle Together 55
 Remembering What You Saw 55
 Vocabulary 56
Filing the Facts Away 57
 Background Research 57
 Instrumentally Speaking 58
 Reaching for New Heights 59
Stepping Across the Curriculum 60
 Language Arts (Writing) 60
 Social Studies 60
 Math 60
Student Activities #9, #10 61-62
Listening to the Music of Liszt 63
 Hungarian Rhapsody No. 2 in
  C sharp minor 63
 Listening Map #7 64
 Liebestraum, Dream of Love 65
 Listening Map #8 66

STRAUSS: THE KING OF
THREE-QUARTER TIME
 Biographical Information 67
Fact Finding As You Watch 68
Putting the Puzzle Together 69
 Vocabulary 69
Filing the Facts Away 70
 Background Research 70
 Instrumentally Speaking 72
 Matching Wits 73
 Reaching for New Heights 74
Stepping Across the Curriculum 75
 Language Arts (Writing) 75
 Social Studies 75
 Musical Experiments (Conducting
  & Dancing) 75
 Creative Arts 76

Student Activity #11 77
Listening to the Music of Strauss 78
 New Pizzicato-Polka, Op.449 78
 Listening Map #9 79
 On the Beautiful Blue Danube, Op. 314 ... 80
 Listening Map #10 81

BIZET'S DREAM
 Biographical Information 82
Fact Finding As You Watch 83
Putting the Puzzle Together 84
 Pull Out the Percussion 84
 Spanish Dances 84
 Vocabulary 85
Filing the Facts Away 86
 Background Research 86
 Fill in the Blanks 87
 Unscramble These Words 87
 Instrumentally Speaking 88
 Higher Level Thinking Skills 89
Stepping Across the Curriculum 90
 Language Arts (Writing) 90
 Math Computation 90
 Social Studies 91
 Creative Arts 91
Student Activities #12, #13, #14 ... 92-93
Listening to the Music of Bizet 94
 The Toreador's Song from
  Prelude to Act I, Carmen, Suite No. 1 ... 94
 Listening Map #11 95
 Farandole from L'Arlesienne Suite, No. 2 .. 96
 Listening Map #12 97
Bibliography 98
About the Author 99
Product Listing 100

JOHANN SEBASTIAN BACH
1685 - 1750

BIOGRAPHICAL INFORMATION:

Johann Sebastian Bach's family was comprised of many talented musicians. At one time, thirty members of the Bach family held organist posts in Germany. Once a year, members of his extended family gathered in Germany to celebrate a day of performing together. Young Bach learned to play the violin at an early age, being taught by his father, and performed for his cousins on these and other special occasions.

Both of Bach's parents became ill and died when he was only nine years of age. Bach's oldest brother, Johann Cristoph, took the boy and a younger brother to live with him, teaching him keyboard skills. He was a quick learner of the clavier, harpsichord and organ, advancing rapidly through the lessons. When Johann Cristoph kept more difficult music from him, Bach copied the music from his older brother's books by moonlight in order to study advanced works on his own.

At age fifteen, Bach went to live at the church of St. Michaels, where he studied music, sang in the church choir as a boy soprano, then later played the viola. By the time he was eighteen years old, Bach was employed as a church organist and orchestral director. Throughout his adult life, Bach had difficulty holding steady jobs, offending people by wanting to do his own music in his own way. He was constantly learning and experimenting with technique, often walking several miles to hear a recital or concert by a famous performer from whom he was influenced.

Married twice, Bach fathered twenty children, of which only nine survived, four of them becoming fine musicians in their own right. He composed more than one thousand pieces of music, many considered 'masterpieces', but was not fully appreciated as a musical genius until long after his death at age sixty-five. Even his own children did not perceive him as genius material, referring to him as a "musical director" to several courts. Now, he is considered to have made the greatest contribution to organ repertoire of any single composer.

FACT FINDING AS YOU WATCH

SCENARIO:

"BACH'S FIGHT FOR FREEDOM"

Video
53 min.

In this story, you will meet a young boy, Frederick Mueller, who serves as an apprentice to one of the most famous composers and musicians ever known. Imagine yourself in the year 1717, having the job of assisting a most disagreeable master for whom you will eventually save the day!

Before viewing this story, tell your classmates about a favorite birthday gift you once received and why you considered it special. After a time of sharing, view the video for the first time, using your research skills to find the interesting facts that follow:

PRIMARY LEVEL:

1. What did Frederick Mueller receive for his birthday? Was it something he really wanted?
   He received a new suit of clothes which he didn't really want.

2. What were some of the tasks Frederick did for Mr. Bach?
   He brought Mr. Bach his meals and pumped the organ for him.

3. What did Frederick want to be when he grew up?
   Frederick wanted to be a stone mason.

4. Who made noise while Bach was composing his music?
   The builders (stone-cutters) made noise.

INTERMEDIATE LEVEL:

1. What was Mr. Bach's "Fight for Freedom"?
   He wanted to work on his own music.

2. Why was Frederick Mueller ashamed of his own father?
   He wouldn't fight injustice.

3. Why was Bach not chosen as the new concertmaster as he planned?
   For political reasons, the Duke chose someone else.

4. How was Bach able to finally escape the authority of the cruel Duke?
   Bach went to work elsewhere.

5. Who eventually stood up to the Duke against his wrong doings in Bach's behalf?
   Frederick's father stood up to the Duke.

PUTTING THE PUZZLE TOGETHER

OBJECTIVES:
1. To identify facts about J. S. Bach as a significant master composer
2. To recognize two famous compositions by Bach
3. To compare customs of Bach's time period with the present
4. To increase the use of vocabulary words and comprehension

DISSECTING THE STORY:
How much of the story about Frederick and J. S. Bach can you recall from your first viewing? As a group, try putting these highlights of the tale in perspective as you use the webbing format below placed on the board or on an overhead projector.

Reproduce BACH Student Activity #1, "Dissecting the Story," pg. 15.

1. What was the setting of the story? Location? Year?
   The story takes place in a castle in Germany in 1717.

2. Who were the important characters?
   The important characters were Bach, Frederick, his parents, concert master, the Duke and Leopold.

3. What was the main idea? Plot?
   Bach was employed by royalty who dictated his actions.

4. Identify the crisis or turning point of the story.
   Bach wanted to change locations in order to do his own music the way he wanted.

5. How was the crisis resolved successfully?
   Frederick and his father helped Bach get away.

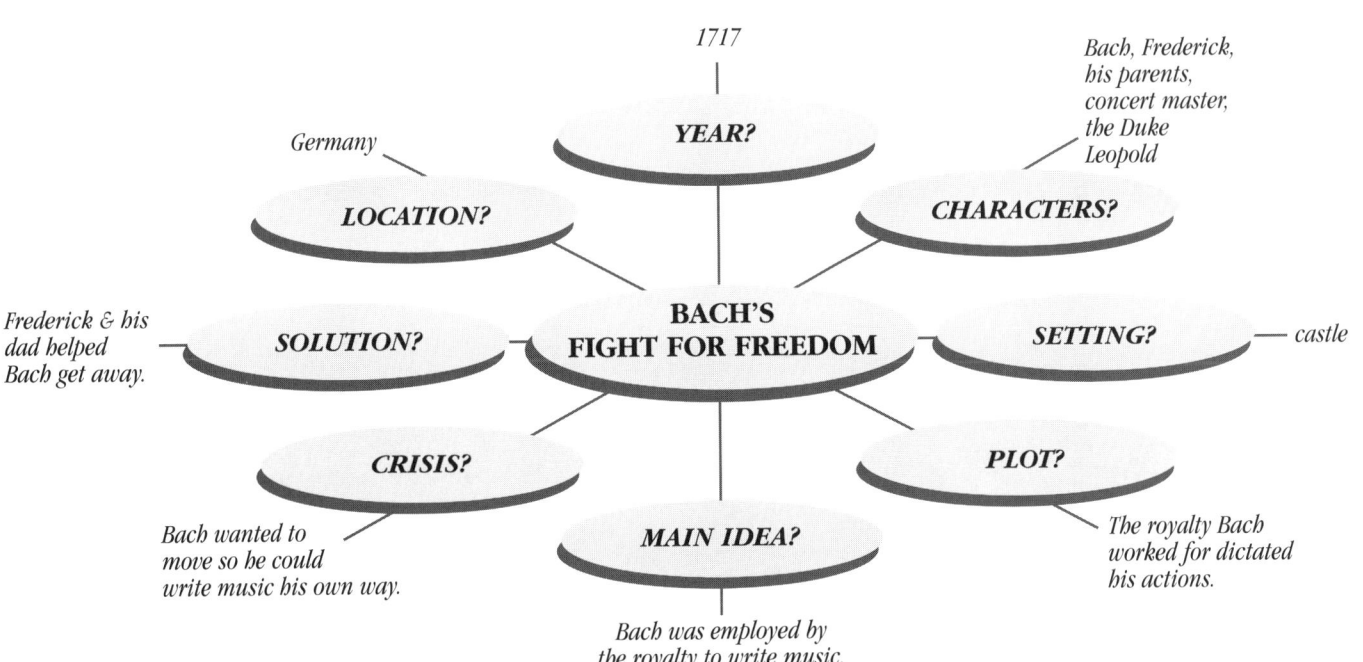

PUTTING THE PUZZLE TOGETHER

VOCABULARY: (PRIMARY LEVEL)

Have students first, put these vocabulary words in alphabetical order on the right, then define each word, using them in sentences of their own.

1. genius
2. servant
3. palace
4. hymn
5. organ

VOCABULARY: (INTERMEDIATE LEVEL)

Have students first, put these twelve vocabulary words in alphabetical order on the right, define each word, decide what part of speech each one is, then use them in sentences of their own. Decide which of these words describe J. S. Bach.

1. genius
2. organist
3. illusion
4. cantata
5. temperamental
6. servant
7. disheveled
8. apprentice
9. hymn
10. scheming
11. harpsichord
12. stonemason

FILING THE FACTS AWAY

BACKGROUND RESEARCH

"The Periods of Music"

The history of music is divided into periods based on the style of music, the history of each era, politics and instrumentation. As you review the categories below, you will notice that **Bach** fits into the period called the **Baroque Era**.

The Renaissance Era (1450-1600) (rebirth)
featuring chants, madrigals, mass and motets
Important Composer: Palestrina

The Baroque Era (1600-1750) (contrast of style)
for church, theater and chamber music
Important Composers: Bach, Handel and Vivaldi

The Classical Era (1750-1825)
art music instead of folk music
Important Composers: Beethoven, Haydn and Mozart

The Romantic Era (1825-1900)
based on the emotions, freeing composers from sacred music's dominance
Important Composers: Brahms, Liszt and Rossini

Twentieth Century Era (1900 to the present)
freed the making of music from most rules of style and technique, becoming more contemporary
Important Composers: Bartok, Copland and Gershwin

Use resources and research materials to find out more about the **Periods of Music** and fill in other important composers for each period for a more complete list.

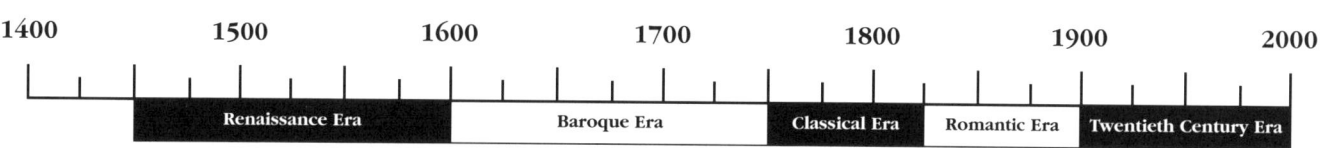

FILING THE FACTS AWAY

TIME TUNNEL

What an exciting story this was about Mr. Bach! Sometimes 'truth' is stranger than 'fiction'! Have the students attempt to put themselves in Frederick's place as they use what was learned to apply to their own circumstances. Can they see why Mr. Bach thought Frederick was assigned to spy on him as he worked? Can they imagine getting dressed up as Frederick did, just to go to work? What if a child had no free time to play and enjoy childhood games and activities? Why did Frederick just accept his own fate? Did Frederick have any musical talent?

Reproduce BACH Student Activity #2, "Time Tunnel," pg. 16.
How many differences did the students notice that compared Mr. Bach's life and time to that of the present day? After some lively discussion, have the students fill in the chart with their own observations about this comparison.

ALL IN A DAY'S WORK

Can you imagine having a 'real' job as a ten year old servant? What jobs would you be able to do well for a demanding task-master? List three tasks Frederick was called upon to do for Mr. Bach as his new servant:

1. *He brought Mr. Bach his meals on a tray.*
2. *He pumped air into the organ.*
3. *He sorted Mr. Bach's music.*

Now list three tasks you are expected to do at home in the present time. Do you think Frederick also had to do chores at home in addition to working for Mr. Bach?

1. *I have to keep my room clean.*
2. *I sort my laundry.*
3. *I take out the trash.*

FILING THE FACTS AWAY

INSTRUMENTALLY SPEAKING: (PRIMARY LEVEL)

Play a game called, **"Find the Maestro"**, by having all children mimic the playing of these instruments for a few seconds; **violin**, **trumpet**, **flute**, **piano**, **trombone**, **cymbals**, **cello**, **drums**, etc., following the teacher's lead. One volunteer is then sent out of the room while a **"Maestro"** child is selected from the group who will lead the charades when "it" returns. The group begins to pantomime, changing instruments each time the **"Maestro"** does, until "it" discovers who the leader is. Choose a new volunteer and continue the game.

INSTRUMENTALLY SPEAKING: (INTERMEDIATE LEVEL)

How observant were you in determining the way musical instruments have changed in appearance and function since the time of J. S. Bach? Wouldn't it be fun to share the instruments of today with Mr. Bach? Answer these questions to see what you noticed:

1. Can you name three instruments Mr. Bach played as shown in this story?
   Mr. Bach played the organ, piano and violin.

2. Who chose the instruments Bach would learn to play?
   His father chose the instruments.

3. What instruments used in the time of Bach are also played today?
   Variations of strings, brass and woodwinds are also played today.

4. What was different about the playing keys of an organ then and now? Why do you suppose that change was made?
   The black and white keys are switched on an organ.

5. What instrument are you learning to play or would like to play someday? Why did you make that choice of instrument for yourself?

FILING THE FACTS AWAY

MATCHING WITS

Reproduce BACH Student Activity #3, "Matching Wits," pg. 16.
Have the students draw a line from the terms in the left column that match words in the right column, giving all words a logical match:

1. J. S. Bach   *stringed instrument* (3)
2. concert master   *keyboard* (10)
3. violin   *masterwork* (9)
4. Frederick   *birthplace* (6)
5. hymn   *father* (8)
6. Eisenach   *Red Palace* (7)
7. Prince Leopold   *church song* (5)
8. Joseph   *scheming* (2)
9. Brandenburg Concerto   *composer* (1)
10. clavier   *apprentice* (4)

REACHING FOR NEW HEIGHTS
HIGHER LEVEL THINKING SKILLS

Stretch your imagination, reaching for answers to these hypothetical questions and prompts in brainstorming fashion. Discuss your brilliant ideas with classmates, listing outstanding ones on the board or chart paper.

1. If J. S. Bach were alive today and came to visit your music classroom as a guest composer, what questions would you want to ask him?
2. List some modern conveniences we enjoy and use today that had not even been invented in Bach's day.
3. Name at least five situations that would never have happened to Mr. Bach but we could experience today. (Ex., a traffic jam)

STEPPING ACROSS THE CURRICULUM

You can extend your interest and knowledge of J. S. Bach and his music into other subject areas with much success. Use the following projects to enrich your study of Bach's "Fight for Freedom".

LANGUAGE ARTS (WRITING)

1. **"WHAT A CHARACTER!"** – Choose one of the characters from this story and write a brief character sketch using several appropriate, descriptive words from this list; loyal, courageous, determined, scheming, brilliant, honest, gifted, mean-spirited, talented, and faithful. Add descriptive words of your own as needed to complete the assignment.

   Make this project a 'guessing game' activity by not revealing the name of the character you wrote about, then have classmates try to guess the person you describe as you read your character's description.

2. **"READ ALL ABOUT IT!"** – Write an interesting newspaper article using one of these headlines as your topic;

   a. "Bach Performs for Prince Leopold at Red Palace!"

   b. "Ten Year Old Helps Bach Escape from Duke Wilhelm!"

   c. "Boy's Father Rips Up Music Composed by Bach!"

3. **"THE PLAY'S THE THING!"** – In small groups, write scripts cooperatively for the 'escape scene' from Bach's story. Include dialogue and action cues for each of the important characters in that scene. Share the scripts by reading the contents for other groups to enjoy.

THEATER ARTS

1. Choose one of the scripts written above, then select a cast of characters including Mr. Bach, Frederick, Joseph, Duke Wilhelm and the concert-master to dramatize the attempted escape scene from the story. (Girls can get into the act, too!)

2. Each of the small groups who wrote these scripts could exchange their work with another group so all students can portray the characters and each group's work would be dramatized.

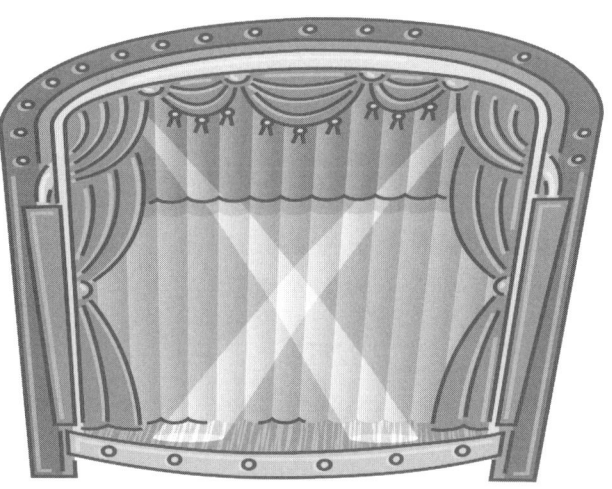

STEPPING ACROSS THE CURRICULUM

SOCIAL STUDIES

Make a comprehensive timeline that highlights significant events in Bach's life. Use research materials in order to find more obscure incidents you might want to include. Start with Bach's birth (1685), death of his parents and going to live with his oldest brother (1694), sent away to school (1700), became organist/orchestral director (1703), married second wife (1721), assumed last full-time church position (1723) and his death (1750) at age sixty-five. Added icons or illustrated milestones would make the timeline more attractive.

CREATIVE ARTS

1. Design and illustrate an original musical instrument, giving it a name and describing its functions, including playing technique and desired sound. Decide which instrument family your new instrument would belong to and why.

   Materials Needed: Drawing paper, pen, pencils or markers.

2. As a group project, make a replica of the Red Palace or a comparable "old world" castle. Use cardboard boxes of various sizes to construct the basic form of the building, then cover with paper mache or decorate with other materials of choice. Make the finished product as realistic and stylistic as possible. Give your castle a name that is symbolic of the design you created.

   Materials Needed: Boxes, paper mache, poster paper, construction paper, glue, scissors, markers and decorative materials.

3. Draw a self-portrait of yourself dressed as in a costume of Frederick's time. Remember to consider how you would dress if you were a servant or if you were wealthy.

   Materials Needed: Drawing paper, pen, pencils or markers.

THE BOTTOM LINE

There is a lesson to be learned from the tale about Bach and Frederick that can be applied in your own life. Discuss which of the following options you think is an appropriate moral of this story?

1. Hardships make a person stronger of character.
2. Music makes one "free."
3. You can't imprison a person's soul.
4. Follow your dream even when the going gets tough.
5. It is hard to be patient while waiting for one's dream to come true.

"The only master you can faithfully serve is your own heart."

BACH Student Activity #1 (Teacher's p. 7)

DISSECTING THE STORY

How much of the story about Frederick and J. S. Bach can you recall from your first viewing? As a group, try putting these highlights of the tale in perspective as you use the webbing format below.

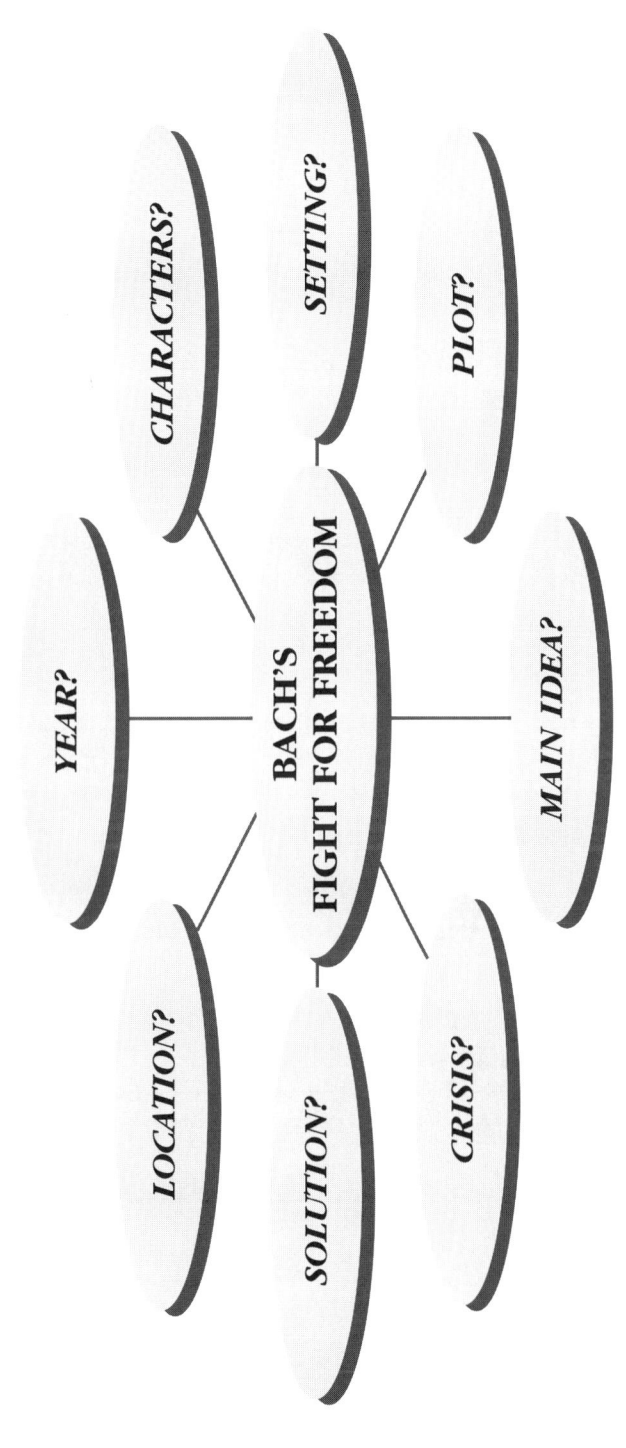

Permission to photocopy the above activity, limited to one school only.

BACH Student Activity #2 (Teacher's p. 10)

TIME TUNNEL

What an exciting story this was about Mr. Bach! Sometimes 'truth' is stranger than 'fiction'! Attempt to put yourself in Frederick's place as you use what was learned to apply to our own circumstances. Can you see why Mr. Bach thought Frederick was assigned to spy on him as he worked? Can you imagine getting dressed up as Frederick did, just to go to work? What if a child like you had no free time to play and enjoy childhood games and activities? Why did Frederick just accept his own fate? Did Frederick have any musical talent?

How many differences did you notice that compared Mr. Bach's life and time to that of the present day? After some lively discussion, fill in the chart with your own observations about this comparison.

TOPIC:	BACH'S TIME:	PRESENT DAY:
Clothing		
Transportation		
Music		
Indoor Lighting		

Permission to photocopy the above activity, limited to one school only.

BACH Student Activity #3 (Teacher's p. 12)

MATCHING WITS

Draw a line from the terms in the left column that match words in the right column, giving all words a logical match:

1. J. S. Bach   *stringed instrument*
2. concert master   *keyboard*
3. violin   *masterwork*
4. Frederick   *birthplace*
5. hymn   *father*
6. Eisenach   *Red Palace*
7. Prince Leopold   *church song*
8. Joseph   *scheming*
9. Brandenburg Concerto   *composer*
10. clavier   *apprentice*

Permission to photocopy the above activity, limited to one school only.

LISTENING TO THE MUSIC OF BACH

SELECTION: *"Overture No. 2 in B minor, Badinerie"* (CD Track #10)
COMPOSER: Johann Sebastian Bach
TIME: 1:24

BACKGROUND:
Bach's *"Suite, No. 2 in B minor"* is capriciously scored for lute and strings. A three-part overture precedes five dance movements; **rondo**, **sarabande**, **bouree**, **polonaise** and **minuet**. To conclude the suite, this *"Badinerie"* provides a merry movement, giving the flute a prominent solo. It is written that the flute was the most popular instrument of German courtiers at the time, due to Frederick the Great's fondness for the instrument.

PREPARATION:
1. Become familiar with the **AB form** of *"Badinerie"* with each section repeated, as the piece moves quickly throughout.
2. In 2/4 time, a skilled flute player is required to play rapid patterns of sixteenth notes in quick succession. Be ready to pat the steady beat (quarter notes) with the right hand on the right knee in this meter (♩ = 96) as you listen to the piece.
3. After you listen to the piece, finding the steady beat, then practice patting the steady beat with the left hand and pat four quick sixteenth notes (♬♬) for each beat with the right hand.

INVOLVEMENT:
1. As they listen to this selection, have the students point to each mark representing a beat as indicated on **Listening Map #1**, patting the steady beat on the knee with the other hand.
2. Practice playing each of the following rhythm patterns repeatedly on suggested metal, percussion instruments after they listen once through: (**finger cymbals**, **triangle**, **cymbals** or **tambourine**)

3. Select volunteers who will add these rhythm patterns one at a time, then two at a time and finally all together to the music.
4. Find out the meanings of these markings; **staccato**, **sharp**, **slur** and **marcato**, locating each one in the printed theme of the A section on **Listening Map #1**.

CLOSURE:
Discuss reasons why an accomplished flute player would want to learn this piece for performance on a concert.

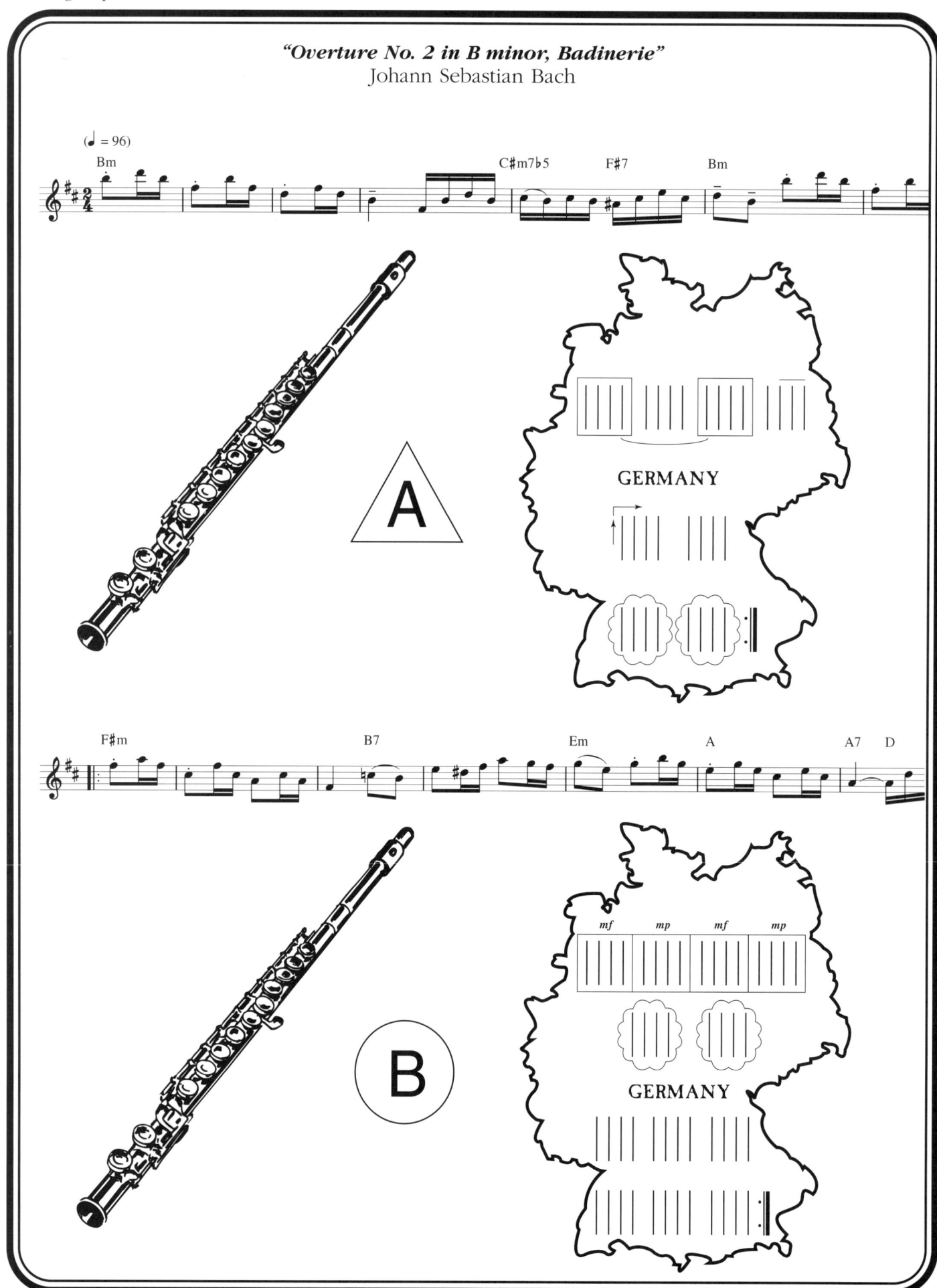

LISTENING TO THE MUSIC OF BACH

SELECTION: *"Overture No. 3 in D Major, II Air"* (CD Track #8)
COMPOSER: Johann Sebastian Bach
TIME: 4:54

BACKGROUND:
Even though Mr. Bach composed four orchestral suites, only two are widely perform today. This *"Air"* movement from *"Suite No. 3 in D Major,"* written for first and second **violins**, **violas** and **cembalo**, is one of Bach's most soulful melodies. Two intertwining melodies played by **violins** are accompanied by a bass pattern played by **viola** and **cembalo** (a stringed instrument similar to a harp).

PREPARATION:
1. As the students listen to this selection, make note that it is written in two distinct sections **(AB form)** with both parts repeated **(AABB)**.
2. To accompany the violin solos, a 'walking bass' pattern of eighth notes is continued throughout, often using octave leaps for emphasis. In the first ending of the A section, the accompaniment utilizes an ascending, step-wise scale pattern.
3. Bach, and many other composers, made use of the "trill", a rapid alternation of two tones, a major or minor second interval apart. In a printed score, the sign *tr* or *tr⌇* is used to signify the use of a trill to the performer.

INVOLVEMENT:
1. Have the students point to the repeat signs on **Listening Map #2**, in order to be ready to return to the beginning of each section quickly as they listen.
2. Keep track of the "walking bass" pattern on **Listening Map #2**, pointing to each note as the line moves. Check the marking of (♩ = 66) on a metronome, which sets the pace for the accompaniment line.
3. With the beat of the bass accompaniment in mind, listen to the piece again and follow the violin melodic solos on **Listening Map #2** as you pat your foot along with the accompaniment.
4. Learn to play a trill on a piano, starting with the lower of the two keys chosen, a second interval apart. Practice for a smooth and even execution of this skill. Find places in Bach's "Air" where trills are played.

CLOSURE:
Discuss your ideas with the class investigating what Mr. Bach was thinking about as he composed this lovely piece. Use descriptive words such as **haunting, yearning, lyrical, soulful** and **eloquent** as important clues to get you started.

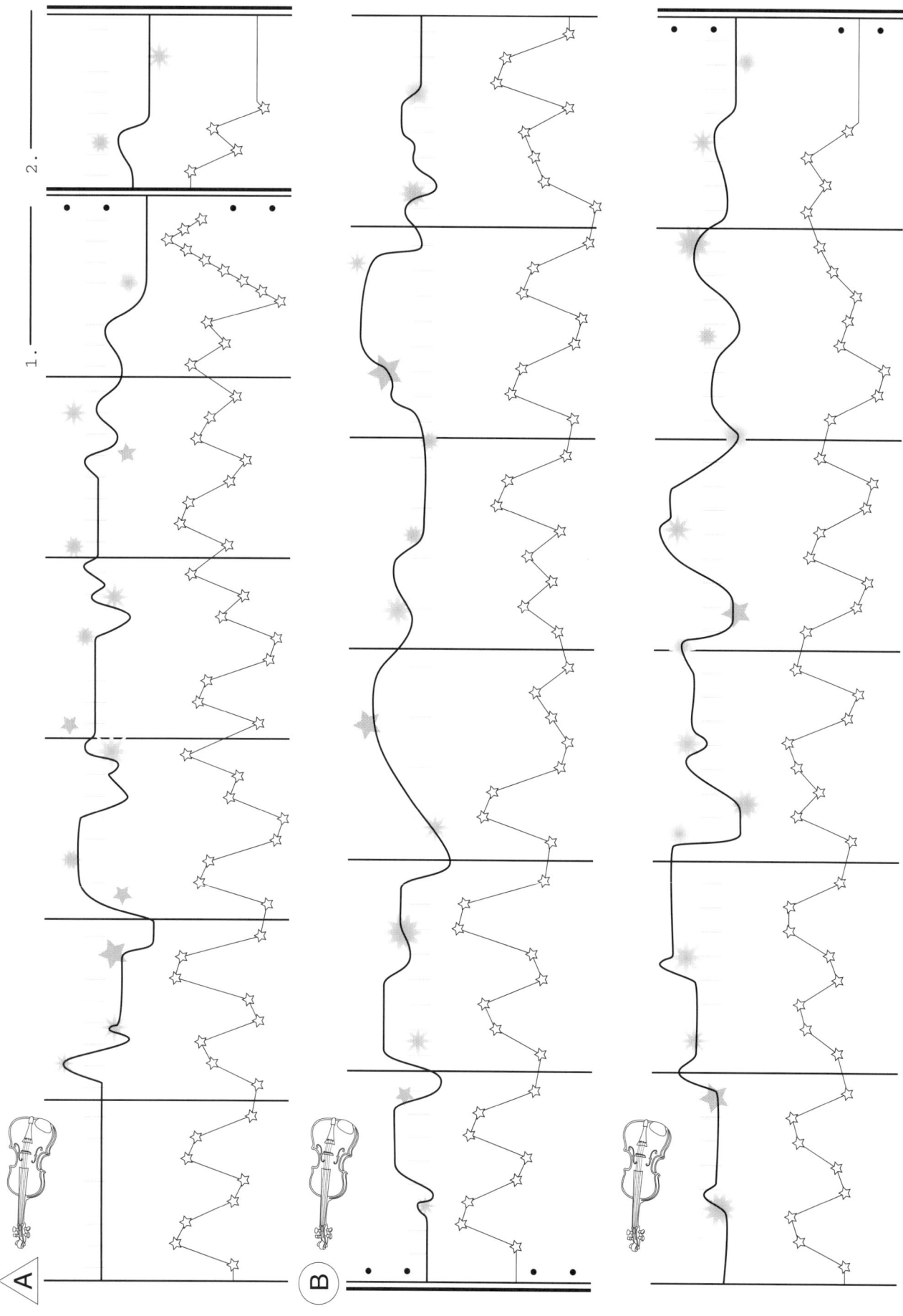

GEORGE FRIDERIC HANDEL
1685 - 1759

BIOGRAPHICAL INFORMATION:

One of greatest composers from the Baroque Era, George Frideric Handel, was born on February 23rd in Hamburg, Germany. His interest in music was manifested at an early age to the extent that he played the organ at the end of church services as a young boy. He also wrote his very first sonata at the age of ten.

His stern father, who was sixty-three years of age when Handel was born, wanted Handel to prepare himself for a more stable career in civil law. Handel smuggled a small keyboard into the tiny attic to practice his music while the family was asleep, against his father's wishes. Soon, the duke heard young Handel play, then persuaded the father to provide proper music lessons for George.

Later, to honor his father, Handel eventually attended the University of Halle for a year to study law, as well as being an organist at the same time. Handel traveled to many European countries, including Italy and England, where he held such positions as organist, teacher, violinist and composer. He actually made his musical reputation far from his original homeland.

Spending many years composing operas in London, his popularity in that field eventually began to diminish. Turning then to the writing of oratorios, Handel directed the performances of his works from the harpsichord, as he played brilliantly. It is said that the keys of his own harpsichord were worn down from long hours of practice.

Having written forty-six operas and thirty-one oratorios, his body of work also includes cantatas, duets, trios, songs and hymns, as well as chamber and orchestral music. His work entitled, "The Messiah" is considered Handel's most famous and beloved oratorio and is still performed frequently throughout the world.

In his later years, Handel's eyesight grew dim until he became totally blind. Still performing, he would be led to the organ by a friend and play majestic works by memory. He died at age seventy-four and was buried in Westminster Abbey, where a monument to his honor, arranged for in his will, stands to this day. He is remembered as the master of the oratorio and for his generosity to those in need.

FACT FINDING AS YOU WATCH

SCENARIO:

"HANDEL'S LAST CHANCE"

Video
51 min.

A young boy named Jamie O'Flaherty, with an angelic face and voice, sings in the marketplace for coins one minute, then helps his young friend steal a plump chicken for their supper the next. As the boys run away from this chaotic scene, trying not to be caught, George Frideric Handel, the famous composer, ends up with the chicken and solutions to the problems at hand.

Before watching this well-told tale, imagine yourself having to use your vocal talent to "sing for your supper". After viewing the video, use your research skills to find the interesting facts that follow:

PRIMARY LEVEL:

1. Why did the character named Jamie not fit in at this new school?
   He was poor and uneducated.

2. Who gave Jamie the nickname of "Mutt" and why?
   Toby gave Jamie this nickname because he was snobbish.

3. Was Mr. Handel rich or poor? How could you tell?
   You could tell Mr. Handel was rich by his clothing and transportation.

4. Why did Jamie help his mother at night and what did he do for her?
   He helped her do laundry.

INTERMEDIATE LEVEL:

1. Explain what is meant by the title, "Handel's Last Chance"?
   His popularity was declining; he needed a good musical work.

2. If Jamie stayed in school, he wanted Mr. Handel to teach him to do something he knew nothing about. What was it he wanted to learn?
   Jamie wanted to learn to read musical notation.

3. What happened to Jamie's mother when he was allowed to go to school?
   She was arrested for not paying her bills.

4. What was kept under Jamie's bed in the boys' sleeping quarters?
   Jamie kept a box with his special things under his bed.

5. How did Mr. Handel happen to hear Jamie singing for the first time?
   He worked at the school.

PUTTING THE PUZZLE TOGETHER

OBJECTIVES:
1. To identify facts about George Frideric Handel as a significant master composer
2. To recognize the most famous oratorio ever composed
3. To distinguish between musical forms
4. To increase the use of vocabulary words and comprehension

"HANDEL" WITH CARE:

As he learned to use his great talent and adjust to an unfamiliar setting, Jamie suffered many embarrassments with great courage and conviction. Discuss the following statements, deciding which are entirely true about him. If you decide a statement is not true, clarify what part is false about it in Jamie's case.

TRUE OR FALSE?

T 1. With limited ability, Jamie was asked to read a passage from a Shakespearean play, in front of his new class.

T 2. Jamie burned a hole in Mr. Handel's choir robe while ironing it for his mother.

F 3. Because he was so exhausted, Jamie sang "out of tune" when he auditioned for Mr. Handel's choir.

T 4. As one of his chores at school, Jamie had to scrub the steps with soap and water as other boys walked by.

F 5. When Mr. Handel invited Jamie to supper, Jamie ate too much, becoming much too ill to perform.

F 6. In frustration, Jamie ran away to sail on the packet-boat but was caught before he could leave.

T 7. Being accused of stealing Mr. Handel's gold pocket watch, Jamie was thrown in jail.

F 8. Through the window of the jail, Jamie's friend got his attention by clapping his hands in a certain way.

PUTTING THE PUZZLE TOGETHER

VOCABULARY: (PRIMARY LEVEL)

Have students first, put these vocabulary words in alphabetical order on the right, then define each word, using them in sentences of their own.

1. opera
2. virtuoso
3. melodist
4. ode
5. harpsichord

VOCABULARY: (INTERMEDIATE LEVEL)

Have students first, put these twelve vocabulary words in alphabetical order on the right, define each word, and decide what part of speech each one is, then choose which of these words describe Mr. Handel.

1. improvisation
2. concerto
3. melodist
4. fugue
5. cantata
6. virtuoso
7. ode
8. harpsichord
9. libretto
10. clavichord
11. opera
12. alto

GETTING A "HANDEL" ON FACTS

BACKGROUND RESEARCH

Many famous stories have been passed down about Mr. Handel and his compositions. Here are some of the most interesting of these tales for you to use in putting together a mental profile of George Frideric Handel. Which ones do you believe are accurate?

"The Wonder Child"

Handel's father, also named George (Georg, Sr.), held the position of barber-surgeon at Saxe-Weissenfels. It was not unusual for young George to travel with his father on his appointed rounds. In 1693, young George went with his father to visit the Duke, who overheard George playing the organ on the premises.

The Duke strongly persuaded old Mr. Handel to let his son pursue the study of music, which the father did against his wishes. Soon the boy was playing the organ at the close of church services to the amazement of all who listened. For one so young with such a marvelous talent, he was nicknamed "The Wonder Child."

1. Was Handel's father right in his wishes to have George study law instead of music?

2. Do you have a special talent that might cause you to be called a "Wonder Child"?

"The Water Music"

Handel made his home in several countries at different times, getting heavily involved in his work and the local scene each time. As a result, he postponed going back to England and his responsibilities there as promised, for a longer period of time than he intended, making the new King of England angry at him.

Upon hearing Handel's music at a service in the Chapel Royal soon after Handel's return, however, the King had a change of heart. In 1717, the King planned a concert on the River Thames, consisting of fifty musicians on a boat, following the King's barge. Music specially written for the occasion by Handel was so loved by the King that he had it repeated three times that evening.

1. Do you think the King's approval of Handel and his music was important? Why?

2. How can music cause someone to have a change of heart?

GETTING A "HANDEL" ON FACTS

"At First Sight"

Handel expected singers who learned and performed his compositions to be able to "sight read" the music or "sing at sight", which means reading the notes for the first time as they sang. As in this video, 'Toby' speaks the famous words that actually may have been spoken years ago by a young printer who applied to sing in Handel's choir.

Handel asked the organist about the availability of any choirmen who "sang at sight" to rehearse some choruses he had just written in great haste. The name of a printer was mentioned who sang in a choir and had a fine voice. However, after several failed tries at singing the prescribed music for a frustrated Mr. Handel, the printer admitted that he could indeed sing at sight, just not at "first sight".

1. What is involved in learning to 'singing at sight'?

2. Was the printer entirely truthful about his musical abilities? Why?

"Hallelujah"

While writing the *"Messiah"*, his best known work, Handel told of having a vision where he saw all of Heaven and a company of angels before him, which inspired him. As a result, the *"Messiah"*, written in three sections, is reported to have been completed in only twenty-three days.

The work was performed first in Dublin in 1742, to raise money for charity and then again in 1743, in England with members of nobility as the appreciative audience. King George, who knew good music when he heard it, was moved and stood up during the singing of the "Hallelujah Chorus". To this day, audiences still stand in tribute to the majesty and wonder of the piece, as did King George long years ago.

1. Is it possible for the *"Messiah"* to have been composed in less than three weeks?

2. Why is the "Hallelujah Chorus" considered one of the most well-known choral pieces ever written?

GETTING A "HANDEL" ON FACTS

INSTRUMENTALLY SPEAKING: (PRIMARY LEVEL)

As a class, brainstorm to name as many musical instruments as you can that are found in an orchestra. Divide the class into four teams, each making a chart, listing those instruments under an assigned 'instrument family' heading of **brass**, **woodwind**, **strings** or **percussion**. Name some characteristics of each particular instrument family indicated by its name. Can you tell which instrument family is not found in a band?

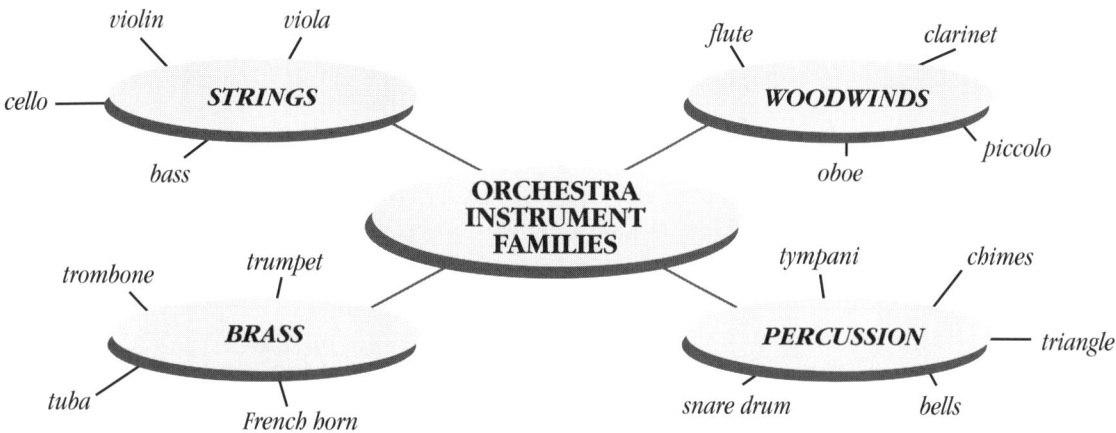

Next, reproduce HANDEL Student Activity #4, "Instrumentally Speaking (Primary Level)," pg. 32. Have the small groups come together to complete this "webbing activity", filling in as many instruments as possible for each family.

INSTRUMENTALLY SPEAKING: (INTERMEDIATE LEVEL)

There are two instruments associated with George Frideric Handel that are used less frequently in performance today and even lesser known. Make it a project to find out all you can about these intriguing instruments and their interesting history of origin.

Harpsichord

The harpsichord, with its unique sound, was designed to look like a small grand piano in shape. The origin evolved from instruments using strings being plucked with a metal quill when a key is depressed (psaltery or dulcimer) instead of being struck with a felt hammer (piano). The result is a more brittle sound than the sound made by a piano.

Even though many compositions were written for the harpsichord as a solo instrument, it didn't have the volume to carry its weight with a full symphony as an accompaniment. Many harpsichords today are ornately painted with additional keyboards and devices used to enhance the dynamics levels. One of the oldest harpsichords made (1521) is now preserved in a museum in London.

GETTING A "HANDEL" ON FACTS

Things to do:

1. Listen to a recording of a harpsichord being played, then compare its sound to that of other keyboard instruments such as an organ and/or a piano.

2. Check out the "Musical Experiments" section of this lesson for a creative way to simulate the sound of a harpsichord.

3. Find information about the earliest origins of harpsichords (14th century) and illustrations of how the instrument has evolved through the years.

Serpent

Handel discovered an instrument called the "serpent" in London and used it in his "Water Music," written in 1717, and again for his "Fireworks Music" in 1749. Made of two shaped pieces of wood joined together, the serpent was designed to play a two and a half octave range.

Created in the 16th century, it was to emulate the sound of a deep bass cornet but was very unreliable in its tone production, leading to a short lived history as an orchestral instrument. Before it fell from use, however, several prominent composers worked it into their compositions.

Things to think about:

Why was this instrument curved like a snake instead of straight?

In which instrument family does the cornet belong? The serpent?

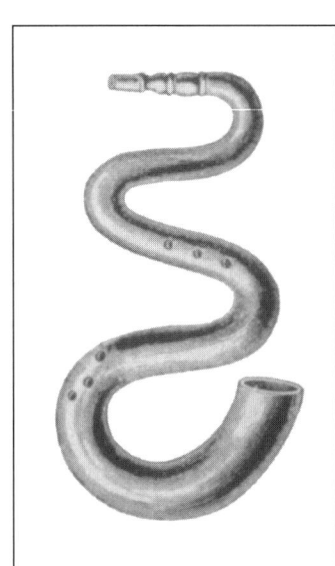

GETTING A "HANDEL" ON FACTS

THE MUSICAL LANGUAGE

At one point in the video, Mr. Handel reminds a singer to soften the voice, telling them to sing "*sotto voce*", a musical term in Italian, meaning 'half-voice'. Handel and other composers use many Italian terms to enhance the performance of their music. Traditionally, Italian is considered the language of music, since most of the musical forms originated in that country. How many of the following commonly used musical terms can you define from the Italian word? Finish the list by looking up the meaning of words you do not already know.

Reproduce HANDEL Student Activity #5, "The Musical Language," p.33.

1. allegro
2. largo
3. legato
4. mezzo
5. piano
6. ritardando
7. staccato
8. vivace

CAN YOU "HANDEL" THESE?
HIGHER LEVEL THINKING SKILLS

1. Handel stated to Dean Swift of the School for Boys that the 'bricks and mortar' of St. Patrick's Cathedral did not impress him at all. What did he mean by that and what do you think did impress Handel about that place where his music was to be performed?

2. Handel was so displeased with the quality of the singers assembled as a choir to perform his new work, he compared them to a variety of animals. Name three animals with coordinating sounds he used to describe those singers. After that, think of three inanimate objects that make equally unpleasant, screeching sounds.

3. Use this list of descriptive words and character traits to apply to the five main characters in this story of "Handel's Last Chance." Add more of your own words as you think of appropriate choices; **aggressive, envious, proud, jealous, loyal, courageous, instinctive, snobbish, honest, greedy, mean, talented, fearful, embarrassed, sneaky, afraid, unfair, astute, hopeful, brilliant and determined**.

Reproduce HANDEL Student Activity #6, "Can You 'Handel' This?" p.33.

STEPPING ACROSS THE CURRICULUM

You can extend your interest and knowledge of George Frideric Handel and his music into other subject areas with much success. Use the following projects to enrich your study of "Handel's Last Chance".

LANGUAGE ARTS (WRITING)

1. Using one of the following options as the main idea, rewrite the ending of this story from a different perspective. What would have happened if . . . .

   - Jamie was actually an untuned singer with no musical talent?
   - Jamie's father was not deceased but suddenly returned home to take care of his family?
   - Handel injured his hand badly and could not direct or play his new composition in Dublin?

2. Handel described himself as a mean and vicious 'ogre'. Now that you know the whole story, write a paragraph describing Handel in the opposite way. What good qualities could you include in your description to make Handel seem like a person others would want to get to know and be around? Tell which description you agree with, in your opinion?

3. There were several 'catch' phrases in this video that have hidden meanings. Turn to a partner and share ideas about what you think the following phrases mean. Write your best ideas down to share with the class.

   - "a noose around the neck"
   - "burning the candle at both ends"
   - "caught dead to rights"
   - "ignoring your true voice"
   - "sink or swim"

4. The words "Handel" and "handle" are called homonyms, words that sound alike, are spelled differently and have different meanings. See how many other sets of homonyms you can list.

SOCIAL STUDIES

1. Using a copy of a map of European countries, locate the important places that became milestones in Handel's brilliant musical career, putting dates in as known. Begin with Halle, Germany, (his birthplace in 1685); then move on to Saxe-Weissenfels (where the Duke heard Handel play); Hamburg (where he was employed as a violinist and harpsichordist at the Opera House); London (where he concentrated on composing operas); Britain (where he turned toward oratorios) and Dublin (where *The Messiah* was first performed).

2. Add other prominent locations as you find their mention in your research about Handel, drawing connecting lines with a dark marker to track his course.

CREATIVE ARTS

1. Collect pictures of musical instruments from old magazines or catalogs. Organize these illustrations into categories based on the **four instrument families**. Divide the class into four groups to work on collages for each family; **brass**, **woodwind**, **strings** and **percussion**. Label each instrument by name and date of origin, if known through research. Display the four collages when finished or make a bulletin board to feature each family one at a time.

   Materials Needed: Pictures of musical instruments, poster board, glue (rubber cement) and markers for labeling.

2. Create a bulletin board area, then select planning committees to design displays, featuring the four instrument family collages above. Each committee would choose one instrument family to highlight with their display, adding any desired decorations as enhancement, with the collage.

   Materials Needed: Background paper or fabric, border trim, cut letters for the title of the display, pins or stapler, collage made by the students and other desired decorations.

3. Make your own original cartoons by illustrating the animals Handel mentioned to describe the out-of-tune singers with which he was confronted before the performance of his music. Add clever captions, using the language Handel might have used, turning your illustrations into cartoons.

   Materials Needed: Drawing paper, construction paper for mounting, pencils, pens or markers.

MUSICAL EXPERIMENTS

The sound of a harpsichord resembles a stringed instrument being plucked. Open the lid of the piano, watching the apparatus inside as it is played. Then, in order to get an idea of this sound, you can change the regular sound a piano makes as it is played, using these two simply alteration techniques (with permission of an authority figure):

1. place a sheet of heavy aluminum foil between the strings and the felt hammers to play the keyboard, or
2. put thumb tacks in the felt hammers, exactly where the hammer will touch the string, then play as usual.
3. Describe the sound of these altered tones as they are produced.

THE BOTTOM LINE

There is a lesson to be learned from the tale about Handel and Jamie that can be applied in your own life. Discuss the following options as an appropriate moral of this story?

1. Do what others tell you.
2. Always listen to your conscience.
3. Believe in yourself.
4. Practice makes perfect.
5. Make others happy by your actions.

*"If you don't believe in yourself,
happiness will always be just out of your reach."*

HANDEL Student Activity #4 (Teacher's p. 27)

INSTRUMENTALLY SPEAKING: (PRIMARY LEVEL)

Fill in as many instruments as possible for each family.

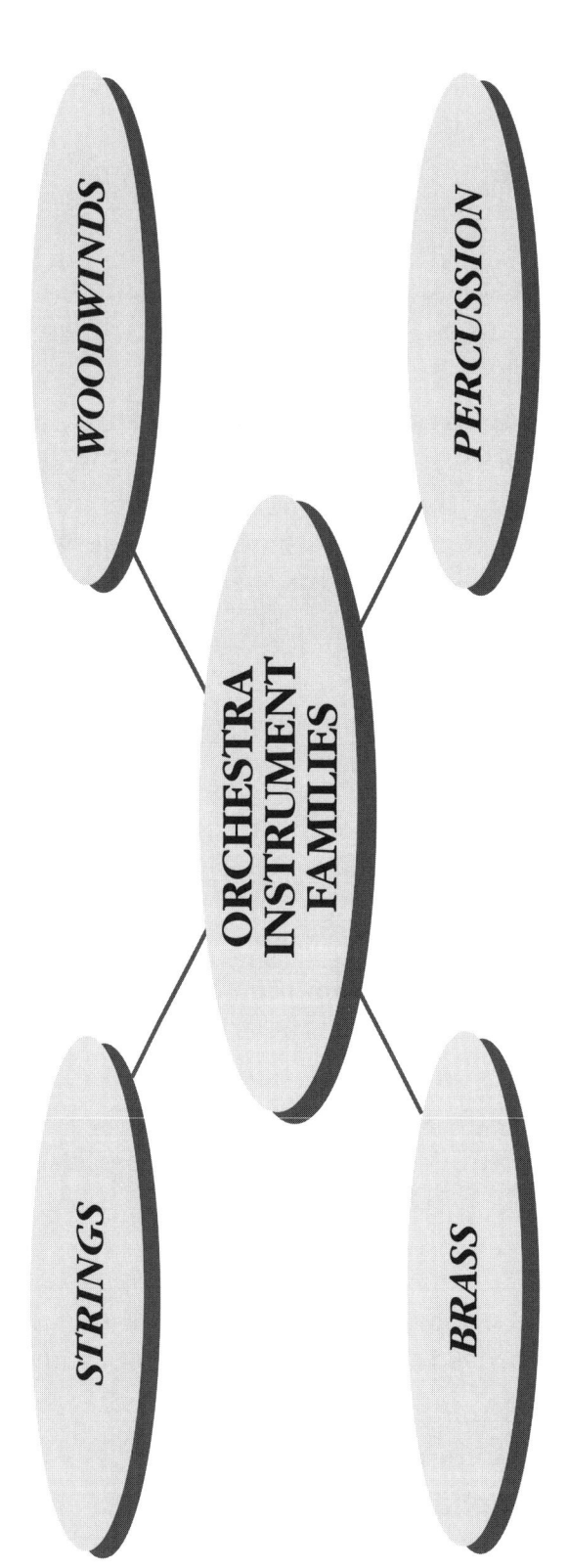

HANDEL Student Activity #5 (Teacher's p. 29)

THE MUSICAL LANGUAGE

How many of the following commonly used musical terms can you define from the Italian word? Finish the list by looking up the meaning of words you do not already know.

ITALIAN TERM	DEFINITION
1. allegro	
2. largo	
3. legato	
4. mezzo	
5. piano	
6. ritardando	
7. staccato	
8. vivace	

Permission to photocopy the above activity, limited to one school only.

HANDEL Student Activity #6 (Teacher's p. 29)

CAN YOU "HANDEL" THIS?

Use this list of descriptive words and character traits to apply to the five main characters in this story of "Handel's Last Chance." Add more of your own words as you think of appropriate choices; **aggressive, envious, proud, jealous, loyal, courageous, instinctive, snobbish, honest, greedy, mean, talented, fearful, embarrassed, sneaky, afraid, unfair, astute, hopeful, brilliant and determined.**

CHARACTERS:	DESCRIPTORS:
1. Mr. Handel	
2. Hugh	
3. Jamie	
4. Jamie's mother	
5. Toby	

Which character rated the most positive traits? _____

The most negative traits? _____

Permission to photocopy the above activity, limited to one school only.

LISTENING TO THE MUSIC OF HANDEL

SELECTION: *"Hallelujah Chorus" from the MESSIAH* (CD Track #15)
COMPOSER: George Frideric Handel
TIME: 3:36

BACKGROUND:
If performed from start to finish, the **Messiah** requires two and a half hours, yet was composed in a short period of twenty-four days. The servants who tried to get Handel to eat and rest during this intense period would often find him in tears as he put the phrases on paper. The **Hallelujah Chorus** is a song of joy, voiced through melodic proclamation in all moving parts. When King George II heard the **Hallelujah Chorus** in 1743, he rose to his feet in respect, a custom that is still observed today as the piece is performed.

PREPARATION:
1. A mixed chorus is made up of four voice parts, two usually sung by females (**soprano and alto**) and two sung by males (**tenor and bass**). Sometimes the soprano part is written for and sung by boy sopranos. Printed music will call attention to this mixed voicing by labeling it **SATB**, going from the highest part to the lowest. What would music labeled **SA** represent? **SSA? TB? TTBB?**

2. An oratorio, like the **Messiah**, is a story set to music, based on a text from the Bible and is performed without costumes, scenery or stage setting.

INVOLVEMENT:
1. The powerful title word, '**Hallelujah**' is used repeatedly in the text of this chorus, sung by each of the four voice parts. As you follow **Listening Map #3**, try counting the number of times the word 'Hallelujah' is heard in the piece. You will notice that sometimes one voice part is singing the word rather quickly while another part is singing it slowly, at the same time. You may need a pencil and paper to tally the score and may not agree with each other on the total.

2. The **Hallelujah Chorus** is rich with contrasts. As you listen again, hold up appropriate prepared cards to signify these contrasts, concentrating on one focus at a time:

Dynamics:	LOUD	SOFT	
Voicing:	WOMEN	MEN	BOTH
Instrumentation:	STRINGS	BRASS	BOTH

CLOSURE:
Decide if Mr. Handel accomplished his goal of proclaiming **praise** in this mighty chorus. Give reasons why this chorus written over two hundred and fifty years ago is still loved and performed.

Listening Map #3

"Hallelujah Chorus from the MESSIAH"
George Frideric Handel

Hallelujah! Hallelujah! Hallelujah! Hallelujah! Hallelujah! Hallelujah! :||

For the Lord God Omnipotent reigneth!
Hallelujah! Hallelujah! Hallelujah! Hallelujah!   *5 times*

The Kingdom of this world is become
THE KINGDOM OF OUR LORD,
AND OF HIS CHRIST . . .

And He shall reign forever and ever!   *4 times*

||: KING of KINGS … forever and ever, Hallelujah! Hallelujah!
and LORD of LORDS … forever and ever, Hallelujah! Hallelujah! :||
KING of KINGS … forever and ever, Hallelujah! Hallelu - jah!
and LORD of LORDS … KING of KINGS and LORD of LORDS
And He Shall Reign …
KINGS of KINGS … forever and ever   and LORD of LORDS …
Hallelujah! Hallelujah! And He Shall Reign Forever and Ever!

||: KING of KINGS and LORD of LORDS :|| And He Shall Reign Forever and Ever!
Hallelujah! Hallelujah! Hallelujah! Hallelujah!

HALLELUJAH!

grand pause

LISTENING TO THE MUSIC OF HANDEL

SELECTION: *"Hornpipe, from the Water Music Suite"* (CD Track #7)
COMPOSER: George Frideric Handel
TIME: 2:56

BACKGROUND:

The **Water Music Suite** was composed by Mr. Handel in 1717, supposedly for him to get back in the good graces of King George I, who was angry at him for being away for so long. This music was performed at a water festival on a barge full of musicians who followed the King's barge down the Thames River.

A 'hornpipe' was a long, thin wooden pipe of an instrument, much like an oboe. A 'hornpipe' is also a term given to a little dance performed by sailors with simple, light steps in a nautical mood.

PREPARATION:

1. As you listen to **Hornpipe**, imagine the piece written for two groups of instruments, one on either side of the King's barge, like in stereo. Notice that the first group makes a stronger pronouncement with more instrumentalists and louder volume, with the second group being more of an echo with fewer players and a softer volume.

2. Practice tapping with the steady beat to find the strong pulse in 3-2 meter. Discuss the meaning of the top number in the time signature (three beats to each measure) and the bottom number (a half note gets a beat.)

THEME:

INVOLVEMENT:

1. Have students follow the beats on **Listening Map #4** as the piece is first heard to get accustomed to the 3/2 time signature and a half note getting the beat.

2. Determine the various note patterns that constitute one measure of music in 3/2 time.

3. Have a volunteer play the three strong beats in each measure lightly on a drum, counting those beats softly as they are played. Choose another volunteer to play six quarter notes per measure on a triangle for contrast, staying in sync with the drum player for stability.

4. Have a group of capable dancers create a 'hornpipe' dance step for both the **A section** and another for the **B section** to perform for the group.

5. As you listen again, name some of the distinctive orchestral instruments heard in each of the two sections of the piece.

CLOSURE:

Determine that the form of "**Hornpipe**" is **ABABAB**, with two sections, each repeated two times with different instrumentation.

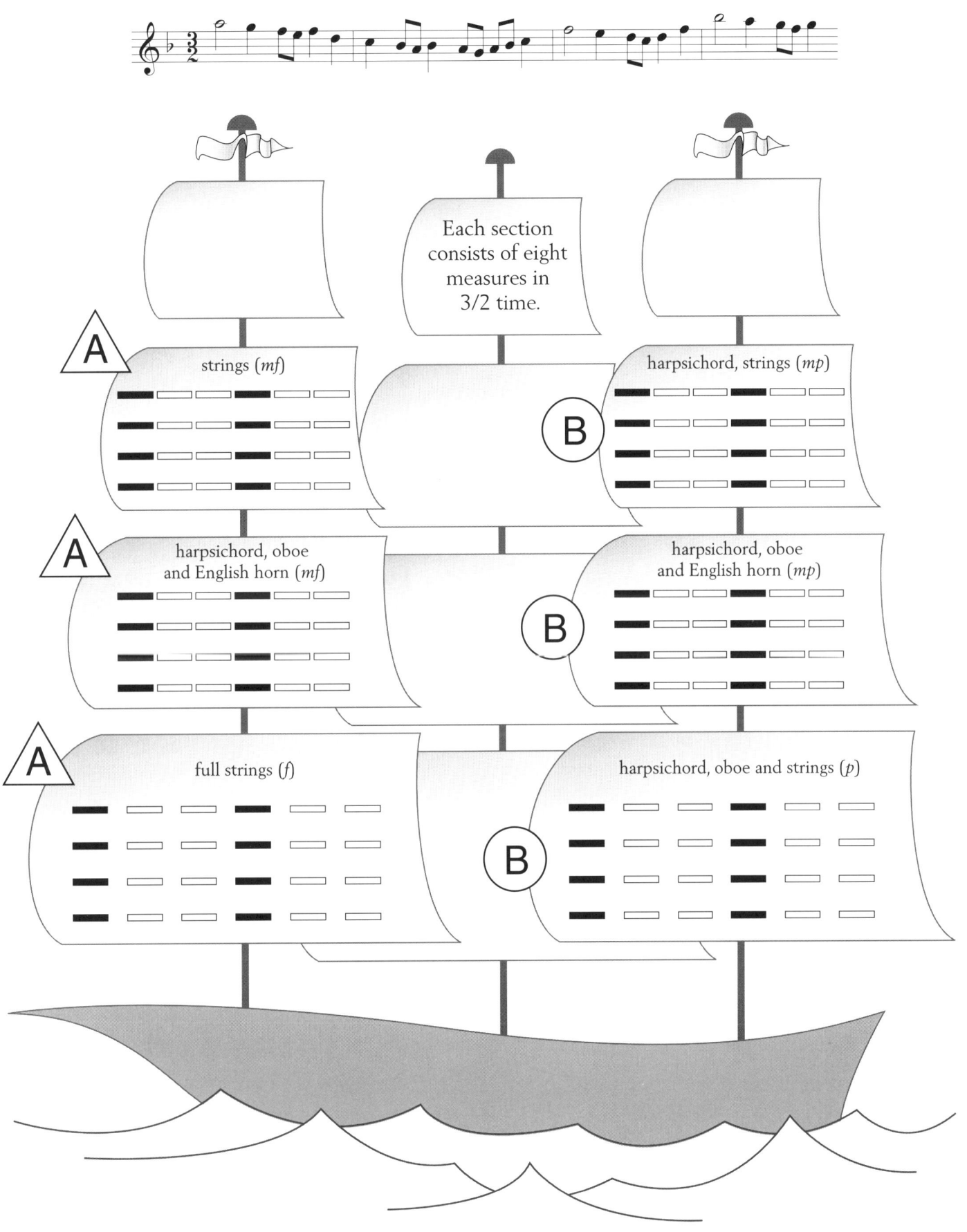

GIOACCHINO ANTONIO ROSSINI
1792 - 1868

BIOGRAPHICAL INFORMATION:

Gioacchino Rossini, was born the son of the town trumpeter in Pesaro, Italy, an Adriatic port. Since he was born on a Leap Year day, February 29th, he only had twenty actual birthdays during his seventy-six years. As a child, Rossini could play the violin, viola and the piano. Before his voice changed, he sang in several operas as a boy soprano.

Rossini began composing music at an early age, writing duets for horn to perform with his father. He began writing operas as a teen-ager, making his debut in 1810 in Venice with a one-act comic opera. By 1813, when he was only twenty-one years of age, he had written seven operas and was gaining recognition in the music world.

Rossini had such a fluent gift for writing beautiful melodies and could complete a work quickly. His opera "The Barber of Seville" (1816), regarded as his greatest operatic work, was written, rehearsed and staged in only two weeks, yet contained six hundred pages of music. It is often quoted that he bragged about being capable of setting even a "laundry list" to music with great success.

Another of his famous operas, "William Tell," was first presented when he was thirty-seven years old. As it turned out, this was also the last opera he ever wrote. By that time, he had plenty of money, world acclaim and a reputation upon which to enjoy the rest of his life. After much international success and recognition, Rossini abruptly retired from composing, writing only insignificant songs during the final thirty-nine years of his life. There are later musical works of his that still have never been published.

Rossini was given several nicknames during his life, based on his music achievements. He was often called "The Swan of Pesaro" because his glowing career brought such positive recognition to that city. The name of "Signor Crescendo" came to him because of the frequent use of a crescendo for dramatic effect in his popular operas. Finally, he was called the "Napoleon of Music" because he took Europe by storm as a musician and composer.

In later years, he fell into ill health and his death came from complications following a heart attack. First buried in Paris, his body was later moved to Florence, Italy, at the request of the Italian government.

FACT FINDING AS YOU WATCH

SCENARIO:

"ROSSINI'S GHOST"

Video
52 min.

An insecure young composer of opera, Gioacchino Rossini, receives encouragement and prophecy from a little girl, Reliana, who magically appears and then disappears as a ghost spirit. Only Mr. Rossini can see this apparition, who brings him an important message from the future when his opera has a curse placed on it and he becomes despondent. The ghost shows Rossini something that changes his attitude about his future as a composer of great opera.

Before watching this intriguing story, imagine yourself being transported into another time period to deliver a life-changing message of hope and courage. After viewing the video, use your research skills to find the interesting facts that follow:

PRIMARY LEVEL:

1. Why did the girl, Reliana, say she hated her best friend, Natalie?
   Natalie was jealous of Reliana and made fun of her.

2. What form of performing did the grandmother do when she was young?
   She was a ballerina dancer.

3. What was in the old suitcase that Reliana's grandmother showed her?
   There were costumes and programs in the suitcase.

4. What kind of animal ran across the stage during the first performance of "The Barber of Seville"?
   A cat ran across the stage.

INTERMEDIATE LEVEL:

1. Who do you think "Rossini's Ghost" actually was?
   The ghost was actually Reliana, as a young girl.

2. Who put a curse on the opera production and how was it broken?
   A jealous performer put a curse on the production.

3. What did the performers offer to do when the opera was almost shut down?
   The performers offered to perform for a cut in pay.

4. What did Rossini do when the first act of "The Barber of Seville" was poorly received?
   He left the concert hall and went home.

5. What was the custom in Italy for people to do to a composer whose work they did not enjoy or appreciate?
   They would go to his home and shout at him from the street.

PUTTING THE PUZZLE TOGETHER

OBJECTIVES:
1. To identify facts about Gioacchino Rossini as a significant opera composer
2. To relate the plot of "The Barber of Seville"
3. To distinguish styles of opera
4. To categorize operatic voicing by range

THE WORLD OF OPERA

The enjoyment of an opera performance is often an acquired taste. The more you know about the plot, production and the music, the more you get out of the presentation. Did you know that there are many kinds of opera? Find out the differences in the following types of opera written throughout music history:

1. **bel canto opera** – with an emphasis on beautiful singing and flexibility
2. **ballad opera** – based on popular songs of the day
3. **grand opera** – dramatic opera in its most sophisticated form
4. **melodramatic opera** – spoofs on more serious material
5. **opera comique** – (comic or buffo opera), a lighter form, most popular in Paris, with witty dialogue and sparkling music

CATEGORIES OF VOICES

Certain operatic roles were written for specific types of singers to portray. To be cast in an opera production meant you had to be a great actor as well as a fine singer. Your vocal range had to fit one of these categories in order to do justice to the performance of the music.

Usually the romantic, lead characters are played by the sopranos (female) and the tenors (male) because of their light quality, depicting goodness and innocence. Altos (female) and basses (male) portray the older characters in a cast, with dramatic basses playing the roles of the villains. Listen to various recordings of operatic performances to become acquainted with the vocal qualities of each category listed here. Learn to label the voices you hear according to these specifications.

RANGE	MALE	FEMALE
Highest	High Tenor (coloratura)	High soprano (coloratura)
High	Tenor	Soprano
Medium	Baritone (bass-baritone)	Mezzo-soprano
Low	Bass (basso profundo)	Contralto (alto)

PUTTING THE PUZZLE TOGETHER

VOCABULARY: (PRIMARY LEVEL)

Have students first, put these vocabulary words in alphabetical order on the right, then define each word, using them in sentences of their own.

1. opera
2. ballet
3. audition
4. curse
5. aria

VOCABULARY: (INTERMEDIATE LEVEL)

Have students first, put these twelve vocabulary words in alphabetical order on the right, define each word, and decide what part of speech each one is, then use each word in sentences of their own.

1. superstition
2. ballet
3. impresario
4. soprano
5. clamor
6. apparition
7. conservatory
8. inherit
9. operatic
10. audition
11. curse
12. aria

FILING THE FACTS AWAY

BACKGROUND RESEARCH

"The Barber of Seville" Synopsis

Act One – Scene One

Young, handsome **Count Almaviva**, and a band of musicians try to serenade **Rosina**, outside the house of **Dr. Bartolo**, who is Rosina's guardian. When she does not immediately appear, **Figaro**, the barber of Seville, enters to assist the Count in his quest for the love of Rosina. Dr. Bartolo keeps a close watch on Rosina, because he wants to marry her himself for her beauty and her dowry. Figaro decides the best way for the Count to see Rosina is to disguise himself as a soldier.

Act One – Scene Two

Rosina admits her love for the Count and prepares a letter to be taken to him by Figaro. A disgraceful rumor about the Count is then started by **Basilio**, the music master, to help Bartolo win Rosina's affections. The Count enters the house disguised as a drunken soldier to meet Rosina. His disorderly conduct gets him arrested but then released when the police realize who he really is.

Act Two

The Count returns to Bartolo's house, disguised as a music teacher, to give Rosina her music lesson. Figaro gives Bartolo a slow shave, affording the young lovers time to plan secretly together. Bartolo then convinces Rosina that the Count is going to give her up so she offers to marry Bartolo at once. Quickly realizing that the Count is her true beloved, she marries him after he gives Basilio an expensive ring to satisfy him and Rosina's dowry to Bartolo, the reward that he wanted all along.

FILING THE FACTS AWAY

FILL IN THE BLANKS:

Using these clues from the word bank below, fill in the blanks based on the story of "The Barber of Seville".

Reproduce ROSSINI Student Activity #7, "Fill in the Blanks," pg. 48.

dowry	letter	Rosina	fraud	music
guardian	Basilio	the Count	wife	barber
soldier	Seville	Rossini	marriage	Figaro

1. This opera, written by **Rossini** takes place in **Seville**.
2. Count Almaviva falls in love with the lovely maiden, **Rosina**.
3. The Count met Figaro, the **barber** of Seville.
4. Figaro helped the Count because he knew Bartolo, the maiden's **guardian**.
5. Since the maiden was not allowed to talk to the Count, she dropped a **letter** from her balcony.
6. The only person allowed to see the maiden was **Basilio**, the music teacher.
7. Figaro told the Count to first disguise himself as a **soldier**.
8. Bartolo discovered that the soldier was a **fraud**.
9. The Count's second disquise was that of a **music** teacher.
10. While Figaro shaved Bartolo, the maiden and the Count made plans for their **marriage**.
11. Dr. Bartolo tried to trick the maiden into being his **wife**.
12. In the end, Bartolo was satisfied to receive Rosina's **dowry**.

UNSCRAMBLE THESE WORDS:

Can you decipher these important people, places or things from "The Barber of Seville"?

Reproduce ROSSINI Student Activity #8, "Unscramble These Words," pg. 48.

1. LELISVE = S E V I L L E
2. IFRGOA = F I G A R O
3. INSISRO = R O S S I N I
4. EBRARB = B A R B E R
5. MLAVAIAV = A L M A V I V A

FILING THE FACTS AWAY

THE CURSE ON THE BARBER OF SEVILLE OPERA

The production of "The Barber of Seville" had two strikes against it from the very beginning. First, an opera based on the same story and with the same title had previously been written by Giovanni Paisello, in 1783. The Italian opera lovers considered the original version a classic and thought Rossini impertinent to use the same material for his opera. Even though Rossini contacted the prior composer to discuss the situation and got full approval from Paisello, who wished the opera well, the audience of opera-goers did not appreciate what happened.

Also, the audience considered Rossini much too young to have any worth as an opera composer and felt he shouldn't be taken seriously as a musician. Their collective minds were made up and their negative response to the first act on opening night put Rossini into deep despair.

Then to make matters even worse, before a note was sung, Rossini entered the performance arena where the audience greeted him with howls of laughing, because of his outfit. The operatic impresario of Naples had talked him into wearing a Spanish officer's uniform with gold braid and ornate buttons, considered most ridiculous by the Italians.

As a final insult, during the first act on opening night, some singers and instrumentalists performed out of tune. A cat unexpectedly scampered across the stage, causing the audience to roar with laughter. The performer playing Bartolo tripped over a trapdoor, crashing to the floor and having to finish the act with a bloody nose. All of these unfortunate incidents were said to be the results of a curse put on the production by a jealous performer.

With the untimely death of the production impresario, the man's wife took over the financial management of the show, cutting the size of the cast and the amount the performers were to be paid.

By the third performance, however, everything went exactly right, causing the audience to embrace the work of Rossini. People then clamored to see "The Barber of Seville" and indeed, still do. No other 'opera comique' has been so popular nor performed more often.

1. What unfortunate incidents happened during the first act of "The Barber of Seville"?

2. What turned the negative response of the audience at the performance into a positive one for subsequent performances?

FILING THE FACTS AWAY

REACHING FOR NEW HEIGHTS
HIGHER LEVEL THINKING SKILLS

Stretch your imagination, reaching for answers to these questions and prompts in brainstorming fashion. Discuss your brilliant ideas with classmates.

1. The female singers in operas are often called "divas" or "prima donnas". Tell what you have learned from the video about the behavior of these elite performers. Find out the names and interesting information about the most famous opera "divas" of all time.

2. Can you name some present day "divas", either in the opera world or in the field of pop music? Which behavior traits of "divas" are the same today as in Rossini's time? Tell who your favorite diva is and why?

3. In the case of many famous musicians such as Gioacchino Rossini, they had the talent to do most of the tasks toward successfully producing an opera. Tell the primary task of each of the following components of an opera production, then decide which of these tasks were most likely done by Mr. Rossini himself.

- composer
- librettist
- arranger
- copyist
- conductor
- set designer
- accompanist

- costume mistress
- diva
- artistic director
- choreographer
- chorus master
- stage manager
- vocal coach

STEPPING ACROSS THE CURRICULUM

You can extend your interest and knowledge of Gioacchino Rossini and his operatic compositions into other subject areas with much success. Use the following projects to enrich your study of "Rossini's Ghost".

LANGUAGE ARTS (WRITING)

1. Work in small groups to write a plot for an original opera. You could borrow topic ideas from mythology, fairy tales, folk tales or make up stories of your own.

   - Create at least three main characters to interact and have dialogue with each other.

   - Decide upon the main idea of your opera, including a crisis and its resolution by the end of the story.

   - Write at least one brief act of actual dialogue, then choose your cast of performers who will sing the dialogue improvisationally.

   - Decide which type of opera your story will most likely fit. (ballad, comic, grand, etc.)

2. Write a descriptive paragraph about Mr. Rossini, including words that paint a picture of this person as a man and as an important composer.

3. Choose two main characters from "The Barber of Seville" and compare their obvious character traits in chart form. Tell which character you would want to perform in this opera if you become a famous opera singer.

MUSICAL EXPERIMENTS

1. Learn to use the technique of the "**crescendo**" for music enhancement as Mr. Rossini did in his music. Pick a familiar song to sing, deciding where a crescendo would be appropriate and practice the effect as a group. If you play an instrument such as piano, recorder or guitar, experiment with using a crescendo as you play. What is the opposite of a crescendo?

2. Discover the present range of your natural singing voice. Starting with Middle C on the piano, sing downward by half steps on a neutral syllable of 'loo', matching tones with the piano sounds as far as you can go. Start again with Middle C, moving upward by half steps, matching the tones as long as you are able. Mark these **lowest to highest pitches** on a piece of **staff paper**. Do you have the potential to be an opera singer someday?

STEPPING ACROSS THE CURRICULUM

THEATER ARTS

1. Design a stage setting for "The Barber of Seville" using a scene for Act One, which takes place outside Dr. Bartolo's home, or inside the home for the other acts. As an option, design a stage set for your own original opera.

   Materials Needed: Drawing paper, poster board, pencils, pen or markers.

2. Perform the original opera acts written above in small groups for your class. Add props, costumes and staging as time permits for rehearsal.

THE BOTTOM LINE

There is a lesson to be learned from the tale about Rossini and Reliana that can be applied in your own life. Which of the following do you think is the true moral of this story?

1. Make as many friends as you can.
2. Try to not hold grudges.
3. Best friends are like money.
4. Always look for the best in people.
5. Good friends don't argue with each other.

"A good friendship just doesn't happen, you must work at it."

ROSSINI Student Activity #7 (Teacher's p. 43)

FILL IN THE BLANKS:

Using these clues from the word bank below, fill in the blanks based on the story of "The Barber of Seville".

dowry	letter	Rosina	fraud	music
guardian	Basilio	the Count	wife	barber
soldier	Seville	Rossini	marriage	Figaro

1. This opera, written by _____ takes place in _____.
2. Count Almaviva falls in love with the lovely maiden, _____.
3. The Count met _____, the barber of Seville.
4. Figaro helped the Count because he knew Bartolo, the maiden's _____.
5. Since the maiden was not allowed to talk to the Count, she dropped a _____ from her balcony.
6. The only person allowed to see the maiden was _____, the music teacher.
7. Figaro told the Count to first disguise himself as a _____.
8. Bartolo discovered that the soldier was a _____.
9. The Count's second disquise was that of a _____ teacher.
10. While Figaro shaved Bartolo, the maiden and the Count made plans for their _____.
11. Dr. Bartolo tried to trick the maiden into being his _____.
12. In the end, Bartolo was satisfied to receive Rosina's _____.

Permission to photocopy the above activity, limited to one school only.

ROSSINI Student Activity #8 (Teacher's p. 43)

UNSCRAMBLE THESE WORDS:

Can you decipher these important people, places or things from "The Barber of Seville"?

1. LELISVE = _ _ _ _ _ _ _
2. IFRGOA = _ _ _ _ _ _
3. INSISRO = _ _ _ _ _ _ _
4. EBRARB = _ _ _ _ _ _
5. MLAVAIAV = _ _ _ _ _ _ _ _

Permission to photocopy the above activity, limited to one school only.

LISTENING TO THE MUSIC OF ROSSINI

SELECTION: "Overture to *Il Barbiere di Siviglia*" (CD Track #1)
COMPOSER: Gioacchino Rossini
TIME: 7:29

BACKGROUND:
Rossini said he composed this entire opera in just thirteen days. The overture was originally written for a work called "Elizabeth, Queen of England," an earlier failure of Rossini's. Rossini thought the work too good to be lost and later made it a success as **The Barber of Seville**," to introduce the opera.

PREPARATION:
1. The overture, preceding an opera, serves to set the mood for the stage production that follows. Often the composer would insert phrases of the most popular melodies from the opera score in hopes that audiences would favorably accept them.
2. Many overtures began with a loud section which called patrons to their seats so the opera could begin, followed by a softer section, allowing people to get settled, ready to listen intently.

INVOLVEMENT:
1. Have the students become familiar with the three melodic themes, being able to recognize each one as they are first introduced in order and later repeated in order.
2. Read and review all the musical terms 'around the house' illustration on **Listening Map #5** to understand the significance of each one throughout this piece.
3. Point to an appropriate term as it is heard in the music. More than one term can be heard at some points. **(NOTE: These musical terms are not listed in listening order 'around the house'.)**
4. Notice that a background accompaniment of pulsing eighth notes is present throughout most of the piece. First tap these eighth notes in the palm, then choose volunteers to play them lightly on rhythm sticks.
5. Tap this rhythm pattern (♫ ♫ ♩ 𝄾) several times, then play the pattern when appropriate on an unpitched percussion instrument of choice.

CLOSURE:
The closing section of this overture is a perfect example of the use of Rossini's crescendo for a dramatic effect. Listen for the rapid phrase repeated and increasing in volume. This is a sample of how the composer got the nickname of "Monsieur Crescendo", during his illustrious career.

LISTENING TO THE MUSIC OF ROSSINI

SELECTION: *"Overture to Guillaume Tell"* (CD Track #8)
COMPOSER: Gioacchino Rossini
TIME: 11:42

BACKGROUND:
This Rossini composition is a showy operatic overture that is still performed often for delighted music lovers. Presented in 1829 to a Paris audience, **William Tell** was Rossini's last dramatic work before he retired at age thirty-nine. At first, audiences didn't like **William Tell** because they considered it too long with boring sections.

Based on a famous Swiss story involving a character named William Tell, who was forced to shoot an apple placed atop his son's head, this opera borrowed its plot from a play written by the author Schiller. Today a statue honoring Mr. Tell and his son stands in the village square at Atsdorf.

PREPARATION:
1. To describe Alpine life, the overture is comprised of four distinct parts; **Dawn** (sunrise in the mountains), **the Storm** (which rises and dies away), **the Calm** (after the storm) and **the Finale** (a spirited march theme).

2. Students will most likely recognize the most familiar themes from the score because this music is often used as the background soundtrack in animated cartoons seen on television and in movies. Anyone who is a fan of the "Lone Ranger" character on radio and television will recognize the final section of the **William Tell Overture** as the memorable theme song for the series.

INVOLVEMENT:
1. Make flash cards or placards with the four important sectional words on them; **Dawn**, **Storm**, **Calm** and **Finale**. Have volunteers hold each card up at the appropriate time using **Listening Map #6**. Make note of the flute cues that separate the sections, such as the raindrops between the first and second sections, and the birds before and after the **Storm**.

2. Describe characteristics of each section after hearing them, such as the **tempo**, **dynamics**, and **primary instruments used** to create the specific moods as titled.

3. Choose a 'lighting' technician who will flick the classroom light switch 'on and off' during the **Storm** section of the piece for a special effect.

4. Choose unpitched percussion instruments to play with the steady beat during the **Finale** section, resting on the interludes as indicated on the Listening Map.

CLOSURE:
In early operatic works, Rossini began to use the technique of rotating fast and slow sections, which composers who followed his influence copied extensively. The **William Tell Overture** is based on this technique, starting with a sunrise, followed by a furious storm, then a pastoral scene and closing with a military brio.

"Overture to Guillaume Tell"
Gioacchino Rossini

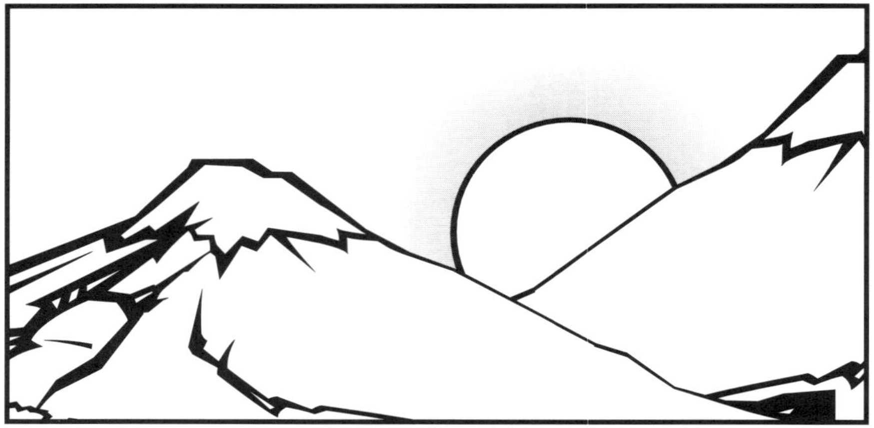

"DAWN"

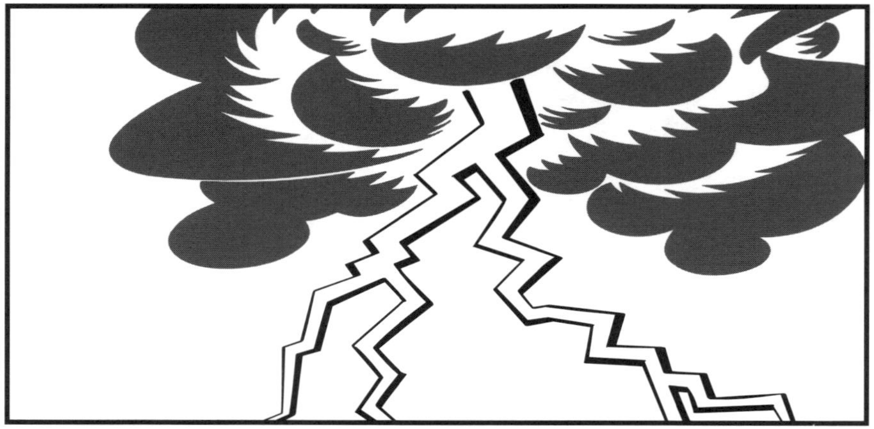

"THE STORM"

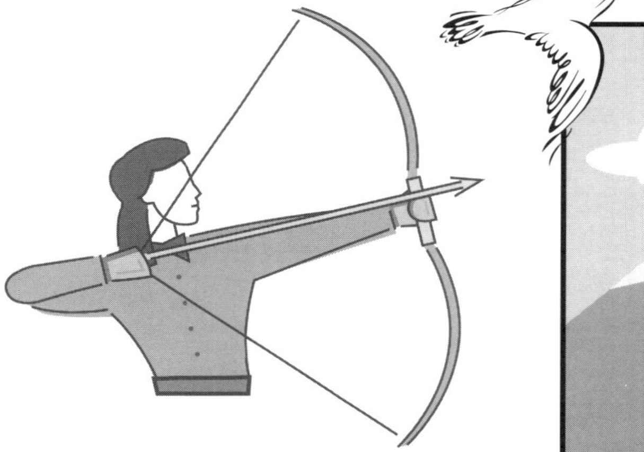

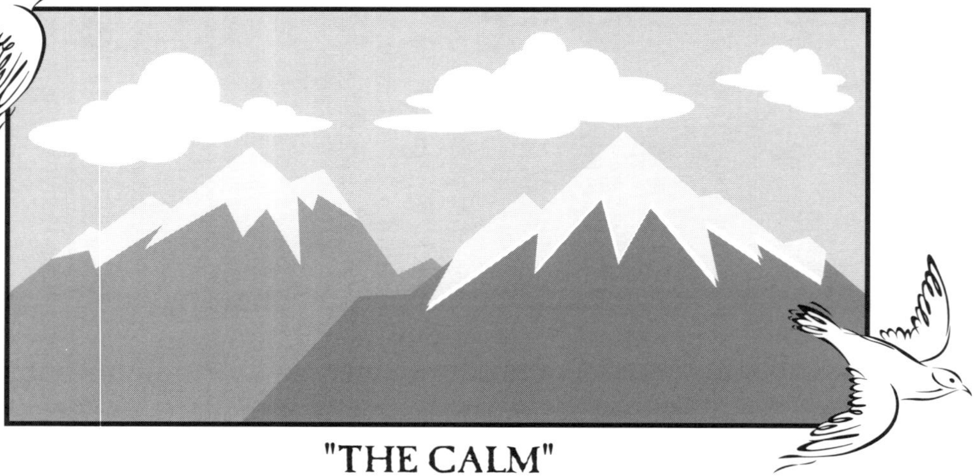

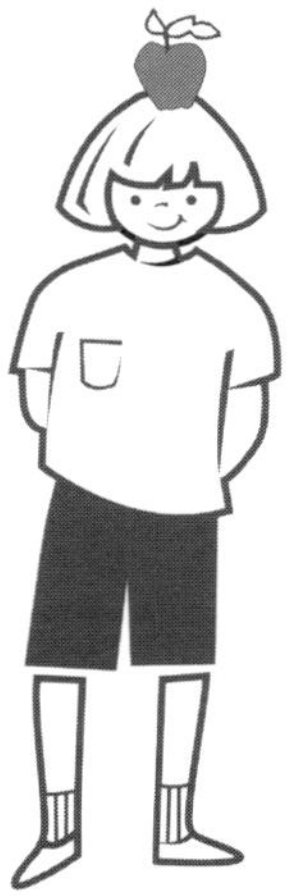

"THE CALM"

INTRODUCTION FOR 9 MEASURES, THEN 16 MEASURES TO PLAY, 4 MEASURES TO REST
soft to loud (four measures), soft to loud (four measures), loud for eight measures
16 MEASURES TO PLAY, 14 MEASURES TO REST
soft to loud (four measures), soft to loud (four measures), loud for eight measures
16 MEASURES TO PLAY (loud), 4 MEASURES TO REST
7 MEASURES IN 4/4, FOLLOWED BY ONE MEASURE IN 2/4
soft to loud (four measures), then loud (three measures)
40 MEASURES TO THE END OF THE PIECE, (RESTING IN MEASURES 25-28)

"FINALE"

Permission to photocopy the above activity, limited to one school only

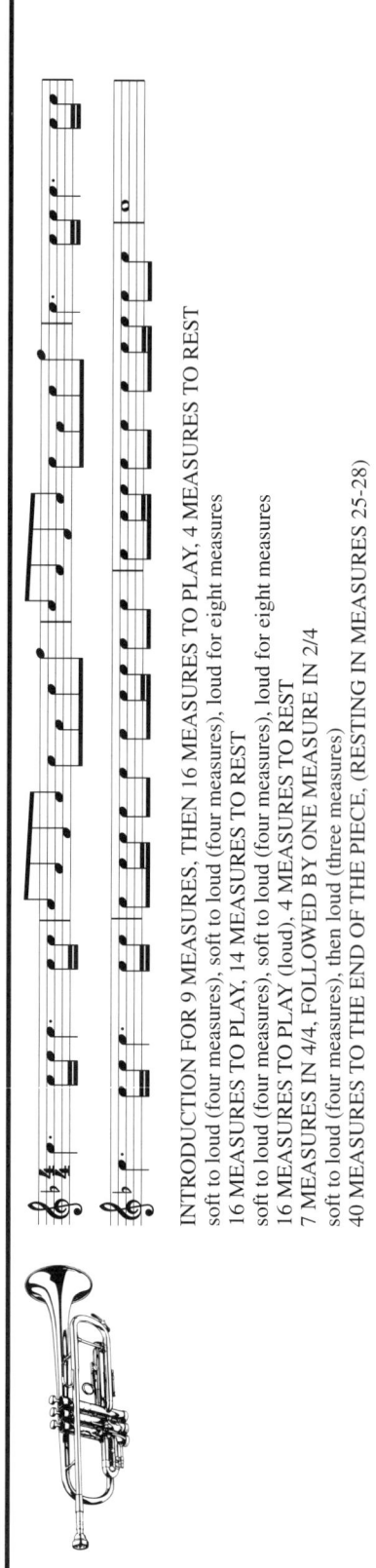

FRANZ LISZT
1811 - 1886

BIOGRAPHICAL INFORMATION:

Born in Hungary in 1811, Franz Liszt was a child prodigy in music. The night he was born, a comet sped across the sky overhead, which some saw as a sign of his greatness to come. He was playing the piano by age seven, composing at eight, making many public appearances at age nine and went to study in Vienna by age ten. His father was a skilled music amateur who played cello in the court orchestra and recognized his son's musical abilities early on.

The family moved to Vienna for Franz to study with the famous piano master, Czerney. After several lessons, Czerney soon refused to take any payment for the privilege of teaching such an outstanding student. In 1823, a concert was arranged which Beethoven, the famous composer, came to enjoy. After Franz performed, it is said that Beethoven lifted him in his arms and kissed him.

At age twelve, Liszt went to Paris to study at the Conservatory. When he arrived, he learned that foreigners were not permitted entrance and that the rules would not be changed, even for such a promising musician. He began to study with outstanding private teachers and presented concerts to great acclaim. A story is reported that he once performed a concerto so well on stage that the orchestra musicians stopped their playing just to listen to him. At age fourteen, he completed work on an opera entitled, "*Don Sanche*" that was only performed twice.

At the death of his father, Liszt gave his fortune to his mother, determined to support himself by teaching privately. Soon after 1830, Liszt met three musicians (Berlioz, Chopin and Paganini) who would soon achieve prominence in the world of music and who inspired Liszt to turn his full attention back to the piano to create his own sensitive music. In 1833, he returned triumphantly to the concert stage, practicing four to five hours a day to prepare.

In England for concert appearances, he stayed a week longer than intended, became ill with pneumonia and died at age fifty-five. In his lifetime, he composed over twelve hundred pieces, invented the 'symphonic poem', which is shorter than a full symphony as it tells a story, and also composed rhapsodies from the songs of the gypsies he heard growing up. Many of the songs he composed are still performed today by serious singers.

FACT FINDING AS YOU WATCH

SCENARIO:

"LISZT'S RHAPSODY"

Video
49 min.

A young, gypsy boy who played the violin beautifully, was brought by Franz Liszt to his grand home as a student, then ended up teaching Liszt an important lesson about his music. Liszt proudly entered the very talented boy in a local music competition that had a most surprising outcome. Do you consider the #13 unlucky?

Before viewing this story, imagine yourself going to live in a strange environment where high expectations are placed upon you to succeed in an unfamiliar setting. After viewing the video, use your research skills to find the interesting facts that follow:

PRIMARY LEVEL:
1. Who first taught the gypsy boy to play the violin so well?
   His grandfather taught him to play the violin.
2. Who went with the boy, Josy, to stay at Liszt's home for his training?
   His grandmother went with Josy for his training.
3. What did Josy do when he got angry at Liszt about the music?
   Josy tried to give his violin away.
4. What was Josy accused of doing, just because of who he was?
   Josy was accused of stealing.

INTERMEDIATE LEVEL:
1. What does it mean that Franz Liszt was his "own worst enemy?"
   He was never satisfied and pushed himself.
2. Why did Josy tell Franz Liszt that the piano was a 'stupid' instrument?
   You couldn't carry the piano with you.
3. How did Josy learn the new music for the competition?
   He learned by ear – by listening to it and playing it back.
4. What did Liszt say had to come out of Josy's prize money if he won the competition?
   Josy had to replace an object he broke.
5. When Liszt told Josy he had practiced enough for the contest, what did Josy do?
   Josy went outside in the dark and practiced some more.

PUTTING THE PUZZLE TOGETHER

OBJECTIVES:
1. To identify facts about Franz Liszt as a famous Hungarian composer
2. To discover the innovative achievements of Liszt
3. To determine how Liszt was true to his heritage
4. To increase the use of vocabulary words and comprehension

REMEMBERING WHAT YOU SAW:

(Reproduce LISZT Student Activity #9, "Remembering What You Saw," pg. 61.)
Think about the story you saw involving the composer, Franz Liszt and the gypsy boy, Josy. Select the best answer from one of the three words below each sentence.

1. Mr. Franz Liszt, famous pianist and composer came from **Hungary**, a European country.
    France   Hungary   Italy

2. Liszt's performance instrument of choice was the **piano**.
    organ   violin   piano

3. Josy, the gypsy boy, was not at all impressed that Mr. Liszt was **rich**.
    rich   smart   talented

4. **Gypsies** considered #13, Josy's number at the music competition, an unlucky number.
    Judges   Gypsies   Liszt

5. Josy told Mr. Liszt the gypsies didn't have much, but they did have **pride**.
    talent   gold   pride

6. His **grandfather** taught the gypsy boy to play the violin so well.
    uncle   grandfather   mother

7. Before he brought the gypsy boy to his home for training, Liszt called him a **beggar**.
    beggar   genius   thief

8. At the music competition, Josy played the music his own way, so he was **disqualified**.
    the winner   a medalist   disqualified

9. Josy told Liszt he didn't need a **judge** to tell him he was the best violinist.
    crowd   judge   teacher

10. When Josy played at Liszt's home for his friends, they played a **duet** for violin and piano.
    duet   symphony   competition

PUTTING THE PUZZLE TOGETHER

VOCABULARY: (PRIMARY LEVEL)

Have students first, put these vocabulary words in alphabetical order on the right, then define each word, using it in sentences of their own.

1. genius
2. recital
3. etude
4. vain
5. duet

VOCABULARY: (INTERMEDIATE LEVEL)

First, put these twelve vocabulary words in alphabetical order on the right, then define each word, decide what part of speech each one is, then use each word in sentences of your own.

1. rhapsody
2. amateur
3. prodigy
4. transcription
5. improvise
6. vain
7. recital
8. arrogant
9. premiere
10. adulation
11. prestige
12. duet

FILING THE FACTS AWAY

BACKGROUND RESEARCH

Liszt's Innovations

Franz Liszt was many things; a composer, a gifted pianist, a teacher and above all else, a showman. During his prolific years in the limelight, he changed the world of performance in several ways that are well documented:

1. **Solo Recital** – Until Liszt came along, a pianist would share a recital or concert with other performers or with an orchestra. Liszt, however, took the spotlight and gave full recitals all by himself with no help whatsoever.

2. **Playing in Profile** – Before Liszt's time, performers on the piano would either face the audience or turn their backs to them as they played. Liszt insisted on playing in profile, turned sideways, so the audience could watch his hands and his face with his long hair swinging to the music.

3. **Lifting the Hands** – Performers, before the time of Liszt, kept their hands close to the piano keys with fingers curled, following the keyboard technique of organists. Liszt liked to raise his hands in a flurry of movement as he played, however, to produce a dramatic effect to the amazement of the audience. Often he would actually startle an audience as his long, flat fingers would fly across the keys.

4. **Transcriptions** – Liszt thought that any piece of music, notated for any other medium, could be performed just as effectively on the piano – by him! Many of his works are actually pieces by other composers, scored for violin or even full orchestra that he would transcribe for only a piano to play. The problem this created was that the works then became too difficult for anyone but Liszt to actually play in performance. Even to this day, many of his transcriptions are not ever played because not many can reach his level of technique and dexterity.

FILING THE FACTS AWAY

INSTRUMENTALLY SPEAKING: (PRIMARY LEVEL)

The young gypsy boy in this story, Josy, was a violin virtuoso even before Liszt tried to teach him. He learned the music, handed down from his grandfather, by listening to it first, then playing it by memory. At one point he threatened to give Liszt his violin when he was very discouraged about trying to learn music another way – Liszt's way, by reading it off a printed page. Did you notice how even Josy's violin sounded screechy when he tentatively tried to read the music, but lilting, like the voice of angels when he played music in his own way?

The Violin

The violin is the smallest instrument in the strings family, making the highest sound of any stringed instrument. A violin player holds the instrument in his left hand, placing the large end under the chin to steady it. With the left hand, the player presses on the strings which raises or lowers the pitch. With the right hand, the player moves the bow across the strings making them vibrate quickly. The sound made by the movement of the strings goes into the body of the violin where it resonates off a sound post, then comes out two carved holes shaped like "f's".

The first spelling of the word violin was *'vyollon'*, dating back to 1505, with the modern spelling not used until the year 1520. The name was derived from the word *'fides'* which means string. There are more violins in a symphony orchestra than any other instrument but it is also important as a solo instrument.

The earliest bow resembled a hunting bow to shoot arrows. It began a little shorter and more rigid than it is today. The ribbon part of the bow that touches the strings is made of horse hair. Other materials have been tried without much success because they lack the required elasticity provided by horsehair coated in resin.

The Triangle

Liszt featured the triangle in his *"Piano Concerto, #1"*, written in 1853. Even though the triangle is the smallest instrument in the orchestra, its sound is distinctive and penetrating, since it is metal striking metal. The triangle may not have actually been triangular in shape when it was first mentioned in the 10th century but trapezoidal with four non-parallel sides.

It was brought to prominence by the Turkish bands in Western Europe. According to size, there are high and low pitched triangles and even tuned triangles have existed. The most common sound, however, is the unpitched ringing sound. Single tones are played on the outside, and tremolos are played by hitting the sides within the frame.

FILING THE FACTS AWAY

REACHING FOR NEW HEIGHTS: HIGHER LEVEL THINKING SKILLS

(Reproduce LISZT Student Activity #10, "Reaching For New Heights," pg. 62.)

1. Pretend you are a composer like Franz Liszt, with many tasks to complete as you bring a new musical composition to the public from start to finish. Place numbers in the blanks below that put together the **correct sequence** from the outset to fruition:

    (4) write out parts for each instrument

    (2) compose the new piece

    (5) add dynamic markings to the score

    (8) conduct the concert performance

    (3) notate the music on manuscript paper

    (7) rehearse the musicians

    (1) originate the melodic theme

    (6) name the composition

2. There are four ways in which aspects of music can change: **dynamics**, **pitch**, **tempo** and **timbre**. Define these words, then use two opposite words to explain their effect on a musical composition. (Example; dynamics = loud/soft)

3. Come up with three descriptive words of your own to describe the sound made by each of the following instruments; **piano**, **violin**, **flute** and **triangle**.

STEPPING ACROSS THE CURRICULUM

LANGUAGE ARTS (WRITING)

1. Choose one of the imaginary topics below and write a paragraph to explain what might happen if . . .
   - a symphony orchestra had no conductor.
   - the orchestra instruments forgot to tune before the concert.
   - a player continued to play wrong notes during performance.
   - the conductor's music blew off the music stand as the orchestra played.
   - the instrument players all switched instruments right before their concert.
2. Read a good biography written about Liszt or other important composers and make an oral report to your class about the important facts you learned.
3. Choose a vocabulary "word of the day" from the list in this lesson, making it your own in both conversation and in writing activities.

SOCIAL STUDIES

1. With your teacher's or parents' help, take a field trip to a live musical concert or opera, then present an illustrated report about your experience.
2. Discuss reasons why we need rules of etiquette for attending a live performance of a play or musical concert. Work in small groups to come up with five reasonable rules to share with other groups about appropriate behavior at public events.
3. Come to an agreement on the five most important rules of etiquette as a class project.

MATH

Write the names of these famous composers on the board or transparency; **Bach**, **Handel**, **Liszt** and **Mozart**. Ask class members to vote on their favorite composer from these choices. Using a student chosen to be secretary, tally the votes as you go. Make a bar graph to show the results of the individual choices.

THE BOTTOM LINE

There is a lesson to be learned from the story about Liszt and Josy that can be applied in your own life. Which of the following do you think is the true moral of this story?

1. If you have a gift, use it.
2. Don't try to be something you are not.
3. When you take pride away from a person, then they have nothing.
4. Always be your own master.
5. Music has no barriers.

"You must bravely face things that come up in your life."

LISZT Student Activity #9 (Teacher's p. 55)

REMEMBERING WHAT YOU SAW:

Think about the story you saw involving the composer, Franz Liszt and the gypsy boy, Josy. Select the best answer from one of the three words below each sentence.

1. Mr. Franz Liszt, famous pianist and composer came from _____, a European country.

    France   Hungary   Italy

2. Liszt's performance instrument of choice was the _____.

    organ   violin   piano

3. Josy, the gypsy boy, was not at all impressed that Mr. Liszt was _____.

    rich   smart   talented

4. _____ considered #13, Josy's number at the music competition, an unlucky number.

    Judges   Gypsies   Liszt

5. Josy told Mr. Liszt the gypsies didn't have much, but they did have _____.

    talent   gold   pride

6. His _____ taught the gypsy boy to play the violin so well.

    uncle   grandfather   mother

7. Before he brought the gypsy boy to his home for training, Liszt called him a _____.

    beggar   genius   thief

8. At the music competition, Josy played the music his own way, so he was _____.

    the winner   a medalist   disqualified

9. Josy told Liszt he didn't need a _____ to tell him he was the best violinist.

    crowd   judge   teacher

10. When Josy played at Liszt's home for his friends, they played a _____ for violin and piano.

    duet   symphony   competition

Permission to photocopy the above activity, limited to one school only.

LISZT Student Activity #10 (Teacher's p. 59)

REACHING FOR NEW HEIGHTS
HIGHER LEVEL THINKING SKILLS

1. Pretend you are a composer like Franz Liszt, with many tasks to complete as you bring a new musical composition to the public from start to finish. Place numbers in the blanks below that put together the **correct sequence** from the outset to fruition:

   _____ write out parts for each instrument

   _____ compose the new piece

   _____ add dynamic markings to the score

   _____ conduct the concert performance

   _____ notate the music on manuscript paper

   _____ rehearse the musicians

   _____ originate the melodic theme

   _____ name the composition

Permission to photocopy the above activity, limited to one school only.

LISTENING TO THE MUSIC OF LISZT

SELECTION: *"Hungarian Rhapsody No. 2 in C sharp minor"* (CD Track #6)
COMPOSER: Franz Liszt
TIME: 9:52

BACKGROUND:
Liszt invented and established the form for a 'rhapsody' and composed twenty Hungarian rhapsodies, incorporating the passion of the Hungarian gypsy melodies and rhythm. Written between 1848 and 1886, these are the works most associated with Liszt.

Originally written for piano alone, the composer orchestrated this version, the most popular of Liszt's works. **Clarinets, violins and violas accompanied by brass** are heard at the beginning during the *lassan* (mournful). A slow first theme gives way to a dance theme, a fast *friskan* movement. The music characteristically becomes faster and louder as it nears the climactic ending.

PREPARATION:
1. From music you have heard and enjoyed, tell how a composer builds an exciting climax within a piece of music.
2. Describe what you would expect to hear in a piece based on Hungarian gypsy influences.
3. Several times you will notice that the full orchestra rests in order to give the spotlight to a solo clarinet player, performing a cadenza. A **cadenza** is an elaborate passage played to bridge one section to another or end a cadence of music.

INVOLVEMENT:
1. Have the students point to each highlight of the piece as they listen, following **Listening Map #7**.
2. Pat the dotted rhythm in the third Listening Map box throughout the music of the next two boxes.
3. On **Listening Map #7**, find where the *Lassan* section ends and the *Friska* section begins.
4. Create a percussion part to be played by tambourines and cymbals during the fast, robust sections, following **Listening Map #7**.
5. Discuss some ways a gifted musician like Franz Liszt could assist younger, aspiring performers.

CLOSURE:
Even though Liszt did not speak the Hungarian language, he brilliantly portrayed the culture in his music, having been greatly influenced by the music of the gypsy people.

Josy was a real person and Liszt wrote about him in his autobiography, "My Life with the Gypsies," published in 1851.

Listening Map #7

"Hungarian Rhapsody, No. 2 in C minor"
Franz Liszt

Lassan section

Start here → drums/cymbals → accelerando → Major to minor → off-beat accents → add more strings → accelerando → oboe/flute dialogue → oboe/strings dance melody → *Friska section* → end of *Lassan* section → to Major chord → fading away → low melody → lower and softer → clarinet duet → clarinet duet with strings → clarinet cadenza → BOOM! → more strings → low melody → mi re do / mi re do / mi re do → clarinet cadenza → even faster → accelerando → flute/clarinet → clarinet cadenza → new melody low strings → melody high strings → dotted rhythm → *f* melody → softer/fast → **BIG LOUD FINISH!** → accelerando → sad farewell → *p* fast → full orchestra with drums → waves of crescendos → full orchestra → fast melody high strings → with cymbals → full orchestra → cymbals → change keys → accelerando → slow melody → descending staccato steps → ha ha, ha ha → ha ha, ha ha → flute choir → *f*

LISTENING TO THE MUSIC OF LISZT

SELECTION: *"Liebestraum, Dream of Love"* (CD Track #3)
COMPOSER: Franz Liszt
TIME: 4:27

BACKGROUND:
Actually Liszt wrote three **Liebestraum** pieces but this appealing third one was adapted from song form to a work for piano, published in 1850. These pieces were all first composed as songs before they were adapted for piano, then later transcribed for orchestra.

PREPARATION:
1. Having been composed first as a song, notice that the theme or recurring melody has a strong vocal quality about it as if it could be performed by a singer.
2. *"Liebestraum"* or *"Dream of Love"* is often played at weddings to set the proper mood for such a ceremony. Give reasons why you think the piece is appropriate for a wedding service.
3. Two examples of Liszt's piano cadenzas are heard in this piece. Find them on **Listening Map #8** before you listen.

INVOLVEMENT:
1. Compare Liszt's *"Liebestraum"* with his popular *"Hungarian Rhapsody No.2."* Tell the major characteristics and moods of both pieces.
2. Determine the absolute pitch names for the six descending, single notes before the first piano cadenza. (E flat, D flat, B, B flat, A flat and G)
3. Point to the numbers around the middle heart-shape with the beat as those measures are played, following **Listening Map #8**.
4. Compare the two piano cadenzas for likeness and difference.
5. Notice how a performer on the piano uses his skills to let the important melody line be heard above full orchestral accompaniment in the third section on **Listening Map #8**.

CLOSURE:
Imagine yourself composing music so difficult that only you could play it! Much of Liszt's music requires a highly skilled and accomplished musician to perform the music on concerts. Also imagine writing all the intricate, rapidly played notes on manuscript paper for other musicians to perform. Liszt's technique was so impressive that he could make a piano sound like a full orchestra all by himself.

JOHANN STRAUSS, JR.

1825 - 1899

BIOGRAPHICAL INFORMATION:

Born in Vienna, Austria, the son of a very famous composer himself, Johann Strauss, Jr., was highly influenced by music at an early age. Johann Strauss, Sr., was the conductor, composer and lead violinist of a dance orchestra whose popularity then could be compared to the rock/pop bands of today. His large orchestra toured Europe extensively and gained recognition as one of the finest dance orchestras of that time.

All this made such an impact on young Johann, for he began learning to play the violin and even wrote his first waltz at age six. The eldest of five children, young Johann was nicknamed "Schani". At the Strauss home, the children were asked to be absolutely quiet while the father worked, forbidden to disturb him in his own suite of rooms.

As his son's talent grew, Papa Strauss soon feared that Johann would one day surpass him in popularity and refused to give any of the children music lessons. In secret, Johann Jr.'s mother, Anna, bought him a violin at age fifteen and provided the lessons to train him. During a visit with his grandmother, he composed his first waltz tune. With the notation written down by his mother, the composition was called "First Thoughts".

When young Johann was seventeen years old, his father left the family, so Johann formed his own orchestra and was a rival of his own father's group. However, when his father died at 1849, the two orchestras merged under Johann's direction. Before long, he had to employ enough musicians for six orchestras to play at several locations at once in the city, just to keep up with the demand for the delightful Strauss music.

Johann gained in popularity as a composer and conductor, being named "King of the Waltz" in many countries, including America, where he came in 1872 to conduct concerts in Boston. He is also known as the inventor of the Viennese 'operetta' that brought the dances of the ballroom to the theatrical stage. Upon his death, the world was saddened and strains of the "Blue Danube Waltz," his most famous waltz, were played in tribute to the great "Waltz King," the king of three-quarter time. He spent his whole life doing just what he loved the most, making people happy through his music.

FACT FINDING AS YOU WATCH

SCENARIO:

"STRAUSS: THE KING OF THREE-QUARTER TIME

Video
51 min.

Needing inspiration for a new musical composition the Countess had requested, Johann Strauss hears the haunting sounds of a hunting horn in the distance that captures his attention. After he meets the boy, Nicholas, who played the horn while riding through the deep woods, they become helpful in each other's lives.

Before watching this intriguing story, imagine becoming rich and famous worldwide because of the music you compose. After viewing the video, use your research skills to find the interesting facts that follow:

PRIMARY LEVEL:

1. Why did Mr. Strauss ask the carriage driver to slow down and stop suddenly in the Vienna woods on the way to the Countess' house?
   He heard a hunting horn in the distance.

2. What was the name of the white horse Nicholas cared for in the stable?
   The horse's name was Lightning.

3. Where did Nicholas keep the hunting horn and who taught him to play it?
   His father taught him to play the hunting horn that was kept buried under the hay in the stable.

4. Where did Nicholas go with Mr. Strauss in the carriage that he had never been before?
   Nicholas went with Mr. Strauss to a public concert.

INTERMEDIATE LEVEL:

1. Why was Strauss called "The King of Three Quarter Time?" What does that mean?
   Mr. Strauss is famous for writing the world's favorite waltzes.

2. What was Strauss hired to do for the Countess? What were her specific instructions to him about the task?
   He was hired to write a new waltz involving nature for the Countess' ball.

3. Why didn't Nicholas' mother stick up for him against his mean stepfather?
   She was afraid of Nicholas' stepfather.

4. What secret is there to be learned about Mr. Blaut, the stable keeper?
   He was a thief.

5. How did Strauss handle the demands of being several places at once to conduct his music?
   He hired others (including his brothers) to help conduct other orchestras.

PUTTING THE PUZZLE TOGETHER

OBJECTIVES:
1. To identify facts about Johann Strauss, Jr., as a major Viennese composer
2. To find out about the talents within a musical dynasty
3. To become acquainted with the waltz as a popular dance style
4. To increase the use of vocabulary words and comprehension.

VOCABULARY: (PRIMARY LEVEL)

Have students first, put these vocabulary words in alphabetical order on the right, then define each word, using them in sentences of their own.

1. encore
2. accent
3. waltz
4. melody
5. debut

VOCABULARY: (INTERMEDIATE LEVEL)

Have students first, put these twelve vocabulary words in alphabetical order on the right, define each word, decide what part of speech each one is, then use them in sentences of their own.

1. modulation
2. encore
3. sensation
4. dynasty
5. waltz
6. lilting
7. ingenuity
8. accent
9. debut
10. operetta
11. lavish
12. melody

FILING THE FACTS AWAY

BACKGROUND RESEARCH

"The Waltz"

ONE – two – three! ONE – two – three! The waltz, a popular dance form, originated in the Enns valley in lower Austria, written in triple time with a strong accent on the first beat of each measure. The term "waltz" came from a latin word, "volvere," that means to turn. Its ancestor, the "landler," was a swirling dance that ended with the girl partners being tossed into the air. The waltz, however, was more refined, using faster, smooth, gliding steps. It was the first dance where partners embraced each other, with sweeping steps that required a joint effort by both partners.

By 1830, Vienna's waltzes were the popular rage in Austrian and German towns. Spreading first through Europe, then on to America, the waltz is still popular today.

Johann Strauss, Sr., named the "Father of the Waltz" and Johann, Jr., known as the "Waltz King," wrote hundreds of popular waltzes. Each composition had originality with a theme all its own. Waltzes are still highly popular today heard in city park festivals, ballroom dance competitions and at lavish balls.

1. Which member of the Strauss family was the most successful and why?

2. Why did the waltz become so popular in its day?

"The Beautiful Blue Danube Waltz"

Johann Strauss, Jr., composed over four hundred waltzes, including the most popular waltz ever written, "The Blue Danube Waltz," which was acclaimed by the whole world. The piece was named for the famous river that flows through Vienna, in honor of the birthplace of Strauss' father, also a famous composer. The waltz was written in 1867, following the battle of Köeniggrätz that put the city of Vienna into sadness and depression.

First performed by a male chorus, it was a moderate failure, but was later rewritten for the Strauss orchestra. Received with much enthusiasm, the waltz became the most requested and the most popular waltz of all time. Actually written as a series of five short waltzes with an introduction, the waltzes are written in different keys with an interlude of modulation between each one.

1. How was the most popular waltz in the world named?

2. Why was this famous waltz a failure at first?

FILING THE FACTS AWAY

"Waltz Wizardry"

Because of the popularity of Strauss and his waltzes, these unique situations happened that have been recorded in music history books:

- The piece given the distinction of having the most requested encores at a concert was the waltz, *"Sinngedicht"* by Johann Strauss II, at the first concert given by the composer at the Dommayer's Restaurant in Vienna in October of 1844. It was played **nineteen times** to end this concert.

- Johann Strauss II, traveled to Boston in June of 1872, to conduct the music for a large event called the 'World Peace Jubilee.' More than two thousand instrument players and twenty thousand singers were assembled there to perform. Strauss is reportedly to have earned $100,000 for conducting this one mammoth performance.

- In 1884, when Strauss had been an orchestra conductor for forty years, a week-long celebration was given him by the people of Vienna. During that time, he was given medals, money and gifts from all over the world. Many great musicians of the time as well as political rulers honored him in generous ways.

    1. What creates an encore at the end of a concert? How many encores are the usual number?

    2. Strauss was not anxious to make the trip across the ocean to America. How was he received once he arrived?

FILING THE FACTS AWAY

INSTRUMENTALLY SPEAKING:

The Hunting Horn/Bugle

Mr. Strauss was immediately drawn to the sound made by Nicholas' hunting horn, played to soothe the beautiful white horse, Lightning, in this story. As Strauss demonstrated in his difficulty to make the desired sound, there is a definite skill to playing this horn, known for its full power and strength.

Horns were first used to signal hunters of prey nearby as its sound flowed from the bell. Instead of just blowing into the horn, one must press the lips close together, getting a buzzing sound as air passes through. From this early ancestry, bugles evolved as horns with no keys to press but with a larger capactiy for tonal range. For horns with no keys, the pitch is changed by changing the position of the mouth and the force of the air.

Nicholas had been taught to play his hunting horn by his father before he died. Nicholas hid the horn because it was special to him and he didn't want it falling into the hands of his stepfather and destroyed.

Fun Things to Do:

1. Practice blowing (buzzing) into the mouthpiece of any brass instrument to experiment with the sounds it will make. Change the shape of your mouth and the amount of air being forced through the mouthpiece to change the pitch you make.

2. Find out the name of the Strauss composition that begins with the sounds of a hunting horn as part of the introduction as played by Nicholas in this video.

3. Name other ways hunting horns or bugles are used prominently today.

The Zither

You may be surprised to learn that hidden within the Strauss orchestra was a lesser known instrument called the '*zither*', used by Strauss for a folk sound. The name '*zither*' comes from the Latin word '*cithara*' and the Greek word, '*kithara*'. The zither is a relative of the dulcimer, having from thirty to forty strings stretched across a flat soundboard and played with a pick or fingers.

Fun Things to Do:

1. If you do not have access to a real zither to play, use an autoharp instead to get a similar sound. Instead of pushing the chordal buttons of the autoharp, just pluck the strings to get the same effect.

2. Make a stringed instrument by cutting a heavy piece of cardboard to the desired shape, cut notches at regular intervals along the top and bottom, then string rubber bands in the notches from top to bottom. Strum or pluck the rubber bands as you sing.

FILING THE FACTS AWAY

MATCHING WITS

Reproduce STRAUSS Student Activity #11, "Matching Wits," pg. 77.
Use a pencil to draw lines from the terms in the left column to words that match in the right column, giving all words the best, logical match:

1. dynasty   *bugle* (6)
2. Anna   *white horse* (10)
3. waltz   *stable boy* (9)
4. Countess   *Blue Danube* (7)
5. Waltz King   *three-quarter time* (3)
6. hunting horn   *bauble* (4)
7. river   *mother* (2)
8. waltz capital   *Strauss* (5)
9. Nicholas   *brothers* (1)
10. Lightning   *Vienna* (8)

FILING THE FACTS AWAY

REACHING FOR NEW HEIGHTS
HIGHER LEVEL THINKING SKILLS

1. A "dynasty" is a group of rulers, statesmen, performers or writers who are all members of the same family. Such is the case of the Strauss family of musicians, who started with Johann Strauss, Sr., then his sons; Johann II, Josef and Eduard and later, even grandsons got into the act. What a family tree!

    Using this chart below of accomplishments involving the Strauss family members, make up a similar chart for members of other musical dynasties such as Bach, Haydn and Mozart.

FAMILY MEMBER NAME	RELATION	NOTED ACCOMPLISHMENT
a. Johann Strauss, Sr. (1804-1849)	Father	"Father of the Waltz"
b. Johann Strauss, Jr. (1825-1899)	Son	"Waltz King"
c. Josef Strauss (1827-1870)	Son	Musician/Composer
d. Eduard Strauss (1835-1916)	Son	Musician/Composer
e. Johann Strauss III	Grandson/Nephew	Musician/Composer

2. Find out interesting facts and chart the accomplishments of modern-day performing dynasties such as the Osmond Brothers, the Beach Boys, the Bee-Gees and the Jackson Five. How do these groups differ from the Strauss family and how are they the same?

3. If your father did not share your enthusiasm for your choice of vocation, would you honor his wishes not to follow your dream, or find a way to fulfill it anyway? Why did Johann Strauss not want his sons to pursue careers in music? How did they all manage to succeed in spite of his lack of support?

4. If you could be the "King" (or Queen) of something important, like the "King of Waltzes", what would you be? List what knowledge, skills and talent you would need to be successful in this quest. Tell how you would get started to receive such positive recognition.

STEPPING ACROSS THE CURRICULUM

You can extend your interest and knowledge of Johann Strauss II and his music into other subject areas with much success. Use the following projects to enrich your study of *"Strauss, the King of Three-Quarter Time."*

LANGUAGE ARTS (WRITING)
Pretend you are Johann Strauss as a young man growing up without your father's approval to be a composer and orchestra conductor. Write a letter to your father, persuading him to change his mind and support you in your choice of careers. Include three main logical points of persuasion.

SOCIAL STUDIES
1. Locate Vienna, Austria, on a European map, pinpointing the Blue Danube River and its tributaries.
2. Estimate how many miles Mr. Strauss traveled on his journey from Vienna, Austria, to Boston, Massachusetts in America.

MUSICAL EXPERIMENTS (CONDUCTING AND DANCING)
1. Strauss changed the rules by often turning to face the audience as he conducted the orchestra instead of facing the musicians. He also would use his violin bow as a baton and danced as he directed. Try your hand at being an orchestra conductor like Johann Strauss! Practice the beat pattern for a waltz as shown below, slowly at first, then faster to be a 'pretend' Strauss family musician.

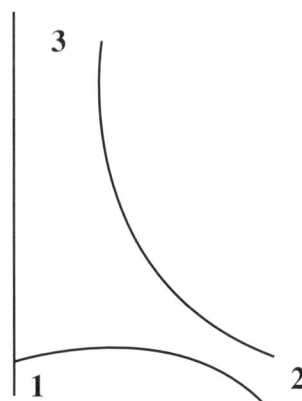

2. Accentuate the first beat of each measure with a stronger motion, as an accent. Learn to use this accent in other ways such as playing a percussive instrument along with a recording, making the first beat louder than the weak beats.

STEPPING ACROSS THE CURRICULUM

3. Learn the waltz dance step that can be done individually or in pairs as you choose. Feel the repeated count of; **1** – 2 – 3, **1** – 2 – 3.

    - Step your right foot to the right side on the heavy beat **1**.
    - Bring the left foot next to the right foot, shifting your weight to the ball of your left foot on beat 2.
    - Shift your weight back to the right foot on beat 3.
    - Repeat these steps to the other side.

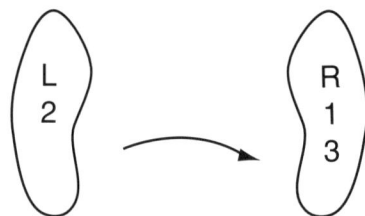

Repeat the above steps forward/backward or side to side. Partners can be facing each other in ballroom style or side by side holding hands.

CREATIVE ARTS

Design a poster or billboard announcing the upcoming concert in your city by the Strauss Orchestra, to be conducted by Johann Strauss II himself. Include important information such as the date, time, place and price of tickets to attend.

Materials Needed: Drawing paper, poster board, pen, pencils or markers.

THE BOTTOM LINE

There is a lesson to be learned from the story about Johann and Nicholas that can be applied to your own life. Which of the following do you think is the true moral of this story?

1. Discover your own talents early in life.
2. Go to family members when you need help.
3. Trust your own instincts in your career choice.
4. Keep trying when things don't work out the first time.
5. The world is meant to be a happy place.

"What we are sometimes most afraid of is our own fear."

STRAUSS Student Activity #11 (Teacher's p.73)

MATCHING WITS

Draw a line from the terms in the left column that match words in the right column, giving all words a logical match:

1. dynasty   *bugle*
2. Anna   *white horse*
3. waltz   *stable boy*
4. Countess   *Blue Danube*
5. Waltz King   *three-quarter time*
6. hunting horn   *bauble*
7. river   *mother*
8. waltz capital   *Strauss*
9. Nicholas   *brothers*
10. Lightning   *Vienna*

Permission to photocopy the above activity, limited to one school only.

LISTENING TO THE MUSIC OF STRAUSS

SELECTION: *"New Pizzicato-Polka, Op. 449"* (CD Track #3)
COMPOSER: Johann Strauss II
TIME: 3:06

BACKGROUND:
To prove that the "Waltz King" could produce more program music than just waltzes, this charming polka is a diversion from his usual compositions. It is performed by the players plucking or pinching the strings of the instruments with the fingers instead of bowing.

PREPARATION:
1. Notice how the melody for this piece is played by the higher pitched strings, accompanied rhythmically by a moving part in the lower strings. In a middle section, the melody is clearly heard played by pitched bells.
2. The polka is a lively peasant dance, originating about 1830 in Bohemia. Dancers of a polka often wear colorful, brightly decorated costumes and headdresses with ribbons.

INVOLVEMENT:
1. Practice gently plucking the strings of any stringed instrument available, such as guitar or autoharp. Refine your technique, making sure you play a definite pitch instead of just a percussive sound.
2. Notice on **Listening Map #9** that the Introduction, **A** and **B sections** are heard repeated during the piece.
3. On melody bells or barred melodic instruments, practice playing the bell part along with the **C section** as shown on **Listening Map #9**.
4. On a contrasting unpitched instrument, have volunteers lightly play this rhythm pattern repeatedly:

CLOSURE:
Give reasons why you think this polka is for dancing or just for listening. Discuss why Mr. Strauss turned from the composition of waltzes to do this and other unique concert pieces.

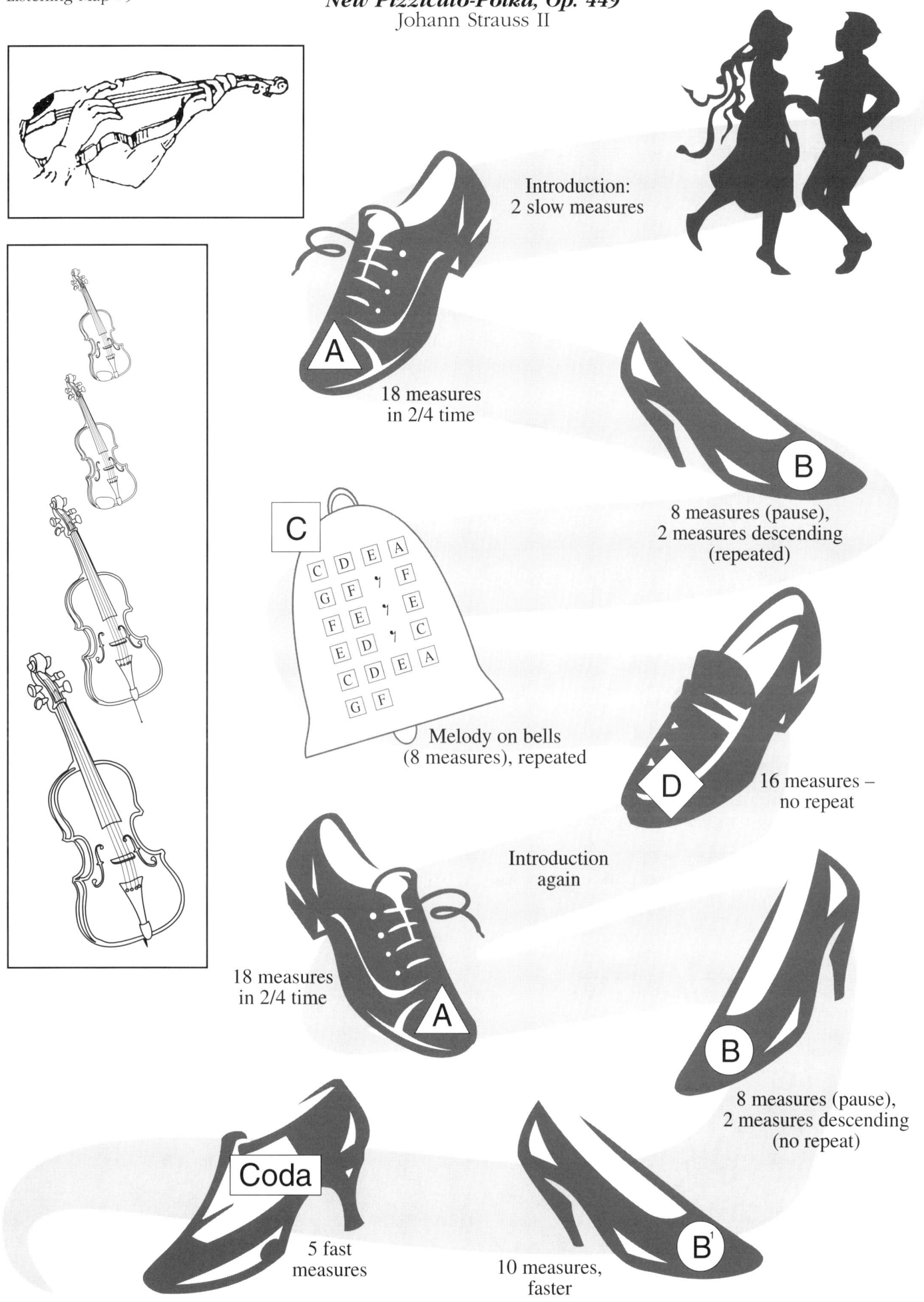

LISTENING TO THE MUSIC OF STRAUSS

SELECTION: *"On the Beautiful, Blue Danube, Op. 314"* (CD Track #6)
COMPOSER: Johann Strauss II
TIME: 9:16

BACKGROUND:
First performed by a male chorus, the **Blue Danube** was a dismal failure. Rewritten as an orchestral waltz, however, it was enthusiastically received. Within a few years of its publication in 1867, over a million copies of the printed score had been sold. The music can be compared to flowing, sparkling water, changing from a rippling brook to a strong, rolling stream.

PREPARATION:
1. Actually, five waltz tunes are put together in sequence to comprise this one most popular waltz by the **Waltz King**. Determine which of the five waltzes take obvious liberties with tempo, giving the impression of twirling and swaying.
2. Listen to discover the two sections that have their own separate, brief introductions.
3. Compare a **waltz** as a dance form to that of a **mazurka** and **minuet**.

INVOLVEMENT:
1. Make five large cards numbered one through five, holding each one up appropriately as each new waltz melody occurs, following the long introduction.
2. Make note of the sections that are repeated in each waltz.
3. Practice each suggested instrumental pattern from **Listening Map #10** separately, then have volunteers add them while listening to the music, using appropriate tempo and dynamic levels.
4. Prepare a dynamics chart, noting the varying levels contained in each section of the five waltzes.
5. Practice a waltz dance step alone or with a partner, moving sharply to the right or left on the first beats of each measure.

CLOSURE:
This music was used as the recurring theme in the movie, "2001, a Space Odyssey", making it popular all over again with a new audience of moviegoers.

GEORGES BIZET
1838 - 1875

BIOGRAPHICAL INFORMATION:

Georges Bizet, born in Paris, showed great musical promise as a young boy. Though actually named Alexandre Cesar Leopold Bizet, the boy's godfather insisted on calling him Georges, which caught on. His father was a teacher of singing and his mother performed piano concerts. At age four, he was taught notes on the piano as he was taught the letters of the alphabet.

Georges entered the music conservatory before he was eleven and won a 'first place' award in a solfege competition before turning twelve. Bizet proved to be a brilliant piano student and composed his own songs for the piano as a young man. In 1935, his exceptional "Symphony in C", written before he was seventeen, was discovered and performed for the first time, to great acclaim.

After such a strong and focused beginning as a musician, Bizet later experienced much disappointment as a composer, with little public acclaim. As a result, he would often abandon projects, for lack of self-confidence. Much of his time was spent trying to make ends meet financially, by teaching piano lessons and writing average pieces he sent to publishers. He refused to perform publicly as a concert pianist, even though he was considered a great performer in his time.

When Bizet was thirty (1868), he still had not produced a single outstanding work that lived up to the promise found in his early years. Soon he gained confidence in himself during the writing of twelve piano duets, *"Jeux d'Enfants,"* five of which were later transcribed for orchestra. Now all he needed was one large-scale success to ensure this reputation as a major composer in France. About this time, he announced a piece he was asked to compose, which turned out to be the turning point in his mediocre career.

"Carmen" became that much-needed success soon after it opened on March 3, 1875. At first misunderstood as strange and dark, the opera later was widely accepted with enthusiasm. Just after *"Carmen"* opened, Bizet became ill from cardiac complications with a recurring throat ailment and died on June 3rd, a broken hearted man. His death, as he was finally coming into his prime as a composer, dealt a heavy blow to French music.

FACT FINDING AS YOU WATCH

SCENARIO:

"BIZET'S DREAM"

Video
53 min.

A young girl, Michelle, who takes piano lessons from an up and coming French composer, Georges Bizet, lets her imagination get the best of her when the plot of his opera becomes entangled with situations in her own family's life. More often than not, there is no concentration on music lessons because of Bizet's preoccupation with his own compositions and Michelle's longing to have her father come home from the army.

Before watching this conflicting story, think of times when you must concentrate on something important but your mind seems to wander where it wants to. After viewing the video, use your research skills to find the interesting facts that follow:

PRIMARY LEVEL:

1. Where was Michelle's father at the beginning of the story?
   He was a soldier in the war.

2. Why was Mr. Bizet usually late for Michelle's piano lessons?
   He stopped to shop and buy desserts.

3. What does Bizet say to Michelle when she makes a mistake at the piano?
   He says, "wrong!"

4. What did Mr. Bizet's next door neighbor do to make his living?
   He was an artist.

INTERMEDIATE LEVEL:

1. Can you explain in your own words what "Bizet's Dream" was?
   He wanted to compose a master work.

2. What does Mr. Bizet hear during Michelle's lesson in addition to the sounds of the piano?
   He hears his own music in his head.

3. Do you think Michelle has any musical talent? How can you tell?
   Michelle has musical talent because she can play with little focus.

4. Why did Bizet abruptly stop going to Michelle's house to teach her piano lessons?
   He wanted to teach in his own home to be near his son.

5. Who were the two suitors for the character, Carmen, in the opera scenes and what were their occupations?
   The two suitors were Don José, who was a soldier, and Escamillo, who was a bull fighter.

PUTTING THE PUZZLE TOGETHER

OBJECTIVES:
1. To identify facts about Georges Bizet as a major French composer
2. To relate the plot of his opera, "Carmen"
3. To create an alternate ending for the operatic story
4. To increase the use of vocabulary words and comprehension

PULL OUT THE PERCUSSION:
Georges Bizet used percussion instruments to bring life to his music and give Spanish flavor to the opera, "*Carmen.*"

Reproduce copies of BIZET Student Activity #12, "Pull Out the Percussion," pg. 92 and have students complete the puzzle.

SPANISH DANCES:
Pictured in the story about Bizet and his opera are Spanish dancers in full costume for you to enjoy. The following dances, originating from that area with a Spanish flair, were derived from the Moors and are known all over the world. Find out more about the following dance forms:

1. **aragonaise** – originating in Aragon
2. **bolero** – a dance done to castanets and lively music in 3/4 time, developed in the 18th century from an old folk dance
3. **fandango** – a fast, lively dance
4. **farandole** – a lively dance in 6/8 time by a winding chain of dancers with joined hands
5. **flamenco** – the Spanish gypsy dance with clapping, heel-tapping stamping of complex rhythms with leaps and turns
6. **habanera** – a slow dance similar to the tango originating in Havana
7. **jota** – a partner dance in 3/4 time with castanets
8. **sequidilla** – a modified version of the bolero

PUTTING THE PUZZLE TOGETHER

VOCABULARY: (PRIMARY LEVEL)

Have students first, put these vocabulary words in alphabetical order, then define each word, using them in sentences of their own.

1. score (musical)
2. fanfare
3. theme (musical)
4. climax
5. dagger

VOCABULARY: (INTERMEDIATE LEVEL)

Have students first, put these twelve vocabulary words in alphabetical order on the right, then define each word, decide what part of speech each one is, and then use each word in sentences of their own.

1. toreador
2. revenge
3. dagger
4. score (musical)
5. virtuoso
6. collaboration
7. brigadier
8. originality
9. fanfare
10. theme (musical)
11. climax
12. prelude

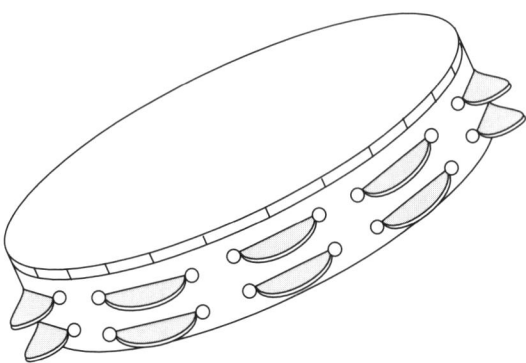

FILING THE FACTS AWAY

BACKGROUND RESEARCH

"Carmen" is one of the most popular operas ever written that contains both 'spoken' and 'sung' dialogue. The female character in Bizet's opera, *"Carmen,"* is one of few exceptions to the operatic rule that the heroine's role must be sung by a soprano. Carmen is played as a sultry gypsy with a rich mezzo voice. The orchestra score is full of original ideas, enabling the orchestra to shine on its own, not just as an accompaniment to the singers. Although composed by a Frenchman, the opera has a Spanish flavor, set in Seville.

"Carmen" Synopsis

Act One

As the story opens, the changing of the guard happens at noon just as the factory workers are taking a break outside. **Carmen**, gypsy heroine of the story, tries to charm **Don José**, brigadier in the Spanish army, who is betrothed to a sweet and lovely **Micaela**. Micaela brings a note from Don José's mother to him, and notices that he has lost his tenderness for her because of Carmen. In a quarrel among the factory workers, Carmen stabs another and is arrested by **Zuniga**, José's superior officer. Carmen manages to have Don José help her escape, for which he is arrested.

Act Two

After he is released from prison, Don José and Carmen meet together at an inn with a band of gypsies. He joins with these vagabonds in dangerous activities, just to be near Carmen. She urges him to come with her to the mountains as he hears the sound of the bugle, calling him back to his quarters. Zuniga, who is also intrigued by Carmen, enters and orders José to return to the barracks. A fight ensues that the gypsies must break up after Don José pulls his sword on Zuniga.

Act Three

Don José is not happy about his way of life since going off with Carmen. She tires of him and transfers her interest to a bullfighter, **Escamillo**. Micaela returns again, begging Don José to return home with her to see his mother, who is ill and dying. He does flee with Micaela to be with his ailing mother but tells Carmen he will return to her.

Act Four

The action takes place at a bullfight where Escamillo arrives with Carmen, who vows to be his. Don José approaches Carmen, begging her to love him but she rebukes him. Carmen runs to the arena gate as she hears the trumpet fanfare to start the bullfight. Don José rushes to her, killing her with his dagger, before Escamillo comes victoriously from the bullring to find her dead.

FILING THE FACTS AWAY

FILL IN THE BLANKS:

Using these clues from the word bank below, fill in the blanks based on the story of "Carmen"

Reproduce BIZET Student Activity #13, "Fill in the Blanks," p. 93.

Carmen	vagabond	escape	dagger
arrested	Bizet	bullfighter	mother
officer	barracks	smuggling	gypsies
brigadier	fanfare	trumpet	swords

1. The opera entitled **Carmen**, was composed by a French composer, **Bizet**.
2. The main character of the story was a **vagabond** who traveled with a band of **gypsies**.
3. The gypsies carried out dangerous acts of **smuggling**.
4. Carmen first gave her attention to Don José, a **brigadier** in the Spanish army.
5. Micaela, a sweet, young woman, tried to win Don José back from Carmen by bringing messages to him from his **mother**.
6. Both Carmen and Don José were **arrested** at different times for different crimes.
7. Don José helped Carmen **escape** after she injured another factory worker, so she can rejoin the gypsies.
8. Zuniga, Don José's superior **officer** ordered him back to the army **barracks**.
9. After Carmen tired of Don José, she transferred her affections to Escamillo, a famous **bullfighter**.
10. Don José and Escamillo fought over Carmen with **swords**, before Zuniga broke it up.
11. A showdown happened at the scene of the bullfight where a **fanfare** is played on a **trumpet**.
12. At the end, Don José stabbed Carmen with his **dagger**.

UNSCRAMBLE THESE WORDS:

Can you decipher these important people, places or things from "Carmen"?

Reproduce BIZET Student Activity #14, "UnScramble These Words," p. 92.

1. EBZTI = *B I Z E T*
2. CMLISEAOL = *E S C A M I L L O*
3. GDREGA = *D A G G E R*
4. LFUBILTGH = *B U L L F I G H T*
5. NCREMA = *C A R M E N*

FILING THE FACTS AWAY

INSTRUMENTALLY SPEAKING: (PRIMARY LEVEL)

Percussion Instruments

Percussion instruments are struck with a mallet or the hand to make their particular sound. Bizet used several members of the percussion family to enhance his opera, "*Carmen*," giving its music a Spanish flavor. Some percussion instruments give out a definite pitch, while others are considered 'unpitched'. Place the following instruments in either a 'pitched' or 'unpitched' category, adding others to the lists as you can:

> **cymbal, snare drum, bell, claves, xylophone, triangle, tambourine, metallophone, castanets, woodblock, quiro, glockenspiel and chime**

Can you think of 'found objects' around the house or tool drawer that would make a percussive sound when struck? Add those items to your list as 'pitched' or 'unpitched'.

INSTRUMENTALLY SPEAKING: (INTERMEDIATE LEVEL)

We can associate two unusual instruments with Georges Bizet by watching this video story and listening to examples of his music. You will most likely already know more about an accordion than you do an English horn.

Accordion (Concertina)

In the video, you see Michelle's mother sitting at a sidewalk café one day, waiting while her daughter takes her piano lesson at Mr. Bizet's house. While there, the mother is serenaded outside by strolling musicians. One of those instruments was an accordion (invented in 1822 in Berlin) or a concertina (invented in 1829).

The main difference in the two instruments is that an accordion has a side keyboard while the concertina has none. Another difference is that the accordion plays one tone as air is drawn out of the instrument and another tone as air is pressed back in. The concertina plays only one sound no matter what is happening to the air in the chamber.

1. Realizing what you now know about the accordion and concertina, which of these instruments did you actually see in the video?
   A concertina was seen in the video instead of an accordion.

2. Can you name the other instrument being played at the café for Michelle's mother?
   A harmonica is seen in the video with the concertina.

FILING THE FACTS AWAY

English Horn (cor anglais)

Bizet, as well as Rossini and other composers, used an English horn prominently in their compositions because of its distinctive, expressive sound. Even though it is neither *English* in origin nor is it a *horn*, the English horn is a double reed instrument pitched lower than an oboe. Often called a 'tenor oboe', with a bulb-shaped bell and bent metal mouthpiece to hold the reed, it has been in the orchestra since the 19th century. It stands out as a solo instrument when a unique sound is required.

1. Name three differences between the oboe and its relative, the English horn.
   The three differences between the oboe and the English horn are: 1) the English horn is pitched lower than the oboe, 2) it has a bulb-shaped bell, and 3) it has a bent metal mouthpiece.

2. To what instrument family does the English horn belong?
   The English horn belongs to the woodwind family of instruments.

HIGHER LEVEL THINKING SKILLS:

1. What are musical 'scales' and why are they so important to musicians, especially students of music? What does it mean to practice scales on the piano in 'contrary motion' as Bizet asked Michelle to during in her lesson? Is there a piano student in your class who could demonstrate this technique?

   Musical scales are series of tones arranged in a sequence of rising or falling pitches contained in one octave. The practicing of scales enables a musician to increase skill and dexterity in singing or playing an instrument. Playing scales in a contrary motion means to start with thumbs or starting fingers together on the home key, then play the scale in one or two octaves with both hands in opposite directions and back again.

2. What did Mr. Bizet mean when Michelle asked him about the lesson she missed and he told her, "I think you just had one?" What lesson did she have?

   The lesson Michelle learned was a lesson about life's relationships instead of a piano lesson.

3. In the annals of music history, Bizet is often thought of as a 'one-work' composer. What does that expression mean? Do you agree with music critics on their opinion?

   A "one-word" composer is a person who is famous in the annals of music history for writing only one famous and lasting composition.

STEPPING ACROSS THE CURRICULUM

You can extend your interest and knowledge of Georges Bizet and his music into other subject areas with much success. Use the following projects to enrich your study of "Bizet's Dream".

LANGUAGE ARTS (WRITING)

1. Choose one of these options to finish the story of the opera, "*Carmen*" and rewrite the ending from another perspective, or create an optional ending of your own:

   - Don José returns home to marry Micaela, forgetting about Carmen entirely.
   - Escalmillo is wounded by Don José's sword during a quarrel for Carmen's love and can't fight the bull.
   - The bull runs out of the ring and chases Carmen because of the color of her dress.

2. Divide these words into syllables, using slash marks, then put the correct number of syllables in the blank following each word. Say each word slowly, clapping each syllable as you speak:

   (example)
   1. OR/CHES/TRA 3
   2. SERENADE _____
   3. VIRTUOSO _____
   4. CONCENTRATION _____
   5. COLLABORATION _____
   6. ORIGINALITY _____

MATH COMPUTATION

These math problems use situations from the opera to create problems you can easily solve. Get some scratch paper and see how quickly you can figure out the process to use each time and then the answers.

1. Escalmillo needed a new red cape to use in the bullring to attract the bull's attention. The heavy fabric for the cape cost $87.00 and the seamstress charged him $25.00 an hour to make the cape that took her three hours in all. What was the total cost of his new cape?

2. The famous composer, Georges Bizet, was born in 1838. In what year did he turn twenty-five years of age?

3. Tickets to attend the opera cost $15.00 for adults and $12.50 for children. How much would it cost a family of five, to attend the performance?

4. Students from three local schools are taking a field trip to see the student performance of "*Carmen*" at the opera house. If school A is sending 317 students, school B is sending 423 students and school C is sending 534, how many students in all are attending the performance?

5. Talented singers auditioned to become part of the chorus to sing for the production of "*Carmen*". A total of 125 singers made the chorus, consisting of 39 sopranos, 27 altos and 37 tenors. How many basses were also picked for the opera chorus?

SOCIAL STUDIES

1. Find Paris, France and Seville, Spain on a map. Establish a route to get from one city to the other as quickly as possible.
2. Compare important customs in each of these cities such as attire, transportation, climate and entertainment as seen in the video about Bizet.

CREATIVE ARTS

1. Make original percussion instruments using 'found objects' from home or school using the suggestions below. Decorate your creations appropriately.

    - Make maracas by putting dried beans or rice into a container with a tight lid.
    - Make tambourines using paper plates with bottle caps attached around the edges.
    - Make drums out of oatmeal containers or coffee cans.
    - Make a bell shaker with 'jingle bells' attached to a strong handle

    Materials Needed: Containers, paper plates, bottle caps, dried beans or rice, decorations, contact paper, construction paper, stapler and glue.

2. Play these original instruments along with recordings of Bizet's lively music to capture the Spanish flavor.

3. Design a flag or banner for Escamillo to carry in victory from the bullfight ring.

    Materials Needed: Drawing paper, pen, pencil and markers.

4. Divide the class into small groups to design and make murals depicting chosen scenes from the opera "*Carmen*". Choose a chairman of each group to keep the group organized and focused toward their goal.

    Materials Needed: Large pieces of white butcher paper, pencils or markers, tempera paints with brushes and acrylic spray to use as a fixative for finished products that will be displayed.

THE BOTTOM LINE

There is a lesson to be learned from the tale about Bizet and Michelle that can be applied to your own life. Which of the following do you think is the true moral of this story?

1. Every story has a happy ending.
2. Opera is not silly and boring.
3. It is always time to learn something new.
4. Life is to be lived!
5. Music helps us sort out our emotions.

"Take control of your life, changing things for the better."

BIZET Student Activity #12 (Teacher's p 84)

PULL OUT THE PERCUSSION:

Georges Bizet used percussion instruments to bring life to his music and give Spanish flavor to the opera, " *Carmen.*" In the puzzle below, find the names of these fifteen percussion instruments; **bass drum**, **bell**, **bongo drums**, **castanets**, **chimes**, **cowbell**, **cymbals**, **gong**, **kettledrum**, **marimba**, **snaredrum**, **tambourine**, **tomtom**, **triangle** and **xylophone**. You can go left to right or down from top to bottom.

```
I A W N D C A S T A N E T S
A T A M B O U R I N E C I W
J O F B X W G M Q T G W T C
D B X C Y B R A H O G D B Y
K E T T L E D R U M S X K M
B L A E O L V I V T S P H B
U L P R P L N M G O N G I A
L S Y F H Q S B X M A W O L
S C T R O M F A K C R I D S
T R I A N G L E U L E M V I
C H I M E S B A S S D R U M
E E Z Q L O A P N Y R H K J
N T M H E F A Z L J U J B G
Z U B O N G O D R U M S K Y
```

Permission to photocopy the above activity, limited to one school only.

BIZET Student Activity #14 (Teacher's p. 87)

UNSCRAMBLE THESE WORDS:

Can you decipher these important people, places or things from *"Carmen"*?

1. EBZTI = __ __ __ __ __
2. CMLISEAOL = __ __ __ __ __ __ __ __ __
3. GDREGA = __ __ __ __ __ __
4. LFUBILTGH = __ __ __ __ __ __ __ __ __
5. NCREMA = __ __ __ __ __ __

Permission to photocopy the above activity, limited to one school only.

BIZET Student Activity #13 (Teacher's p. 87)

FILL IN THE BLANKS:

Using these clues from the word bank below, fill in the blanks based on the story of "Carmen."

Carmen	vagabond	escape	dagger
arrested	Bizet	bullfighter	mother
officer	barracks	smuggling	gypsies
brigadier	fanfare	trumpet	swords

1. The opera entitled _____, was composed by a French composer, _____.

2. The main character of the story was a _____ who traveled with a band of _____.

3. The gypsies carried out dangerous acts of _____.

4. Carmen first gave her attention to Don José, a _____ in the Spanish army.

5. Micaela, a sweet, young woman, tried to win Don José back from Carmen by bringing messages to him from his _____.

6. Both Carmen and Don José were _____ at different times for different crimes.

7. Don José helped Carmen _____ after she injured another factory worker, so she can rejoin the gypsies.

8. Zuniga, Don José's superior _____, ordered him back to the army _____.

9. After Carmen tired of Don José, she transfered her affections to Escamillo, a famous _____.

10. Don José and Escamillo fought over Carmen with _____, before Zuniga broke it up.

11. A showdown happened at the scene of the bullfight where a _____ is played on a _____.

12. At the end, Don José stabbed Carmen with his _____.

Permission to photocopy the above activity, limited to one school only.

LISTENING TO THE MUSIC OF BIZET

SELECTION: *"The Toreador's Song from Prelude to Act I, Carmen, Suite No. 1"* (CD track #5)

COMPOSER: Georges Bizet

TIME: 2:14

BACKGROUND:

Even though he was a Frenchman, Mr. Bizet brought the color and flair of Spain to his popular opera, *"Carmen."* This toreador theme makes use of exciting rhythms indicative of the gypsy influence which is prominent in the story line.

PREPARATION:

1. Discover that this piece is written in Rondo form **(ABACA)** with an exciting, recurring theme **(A)** played loudly, accented with cymbal crashes.

2. Bizet made use of a tremolo effect on the strings to add suspense to a particular movement as the tone is sustained. Listen for this tremolo effect (a quivering, fluttering, unsteady tone produced by rapid alternation of down-bow and up-bow) in dramatic passages.

3. Recognize and list instruments from the percussion family that Bizet used to add a Spanish flair to his music.

INVOLVEMENT:

1. As they follow **Listening Map #11**, have students raise their hands during the **C section** to signify when they will stop marching in place and begin to move about. They can either count the measures or listen for the exciting crescendo as their signal.

2. Practice playing the cymbals on marked beats in the **A section** each time, noticing that the ending is slightly different. Have volunteers then play with the recording, using **Listening Map #11** as their guide.

3. Practice playing the triangle as marked on **Listening Map #11** during the **B section** of the rondo. Start softly, building a crescendo toward the climax of the section. Tap the side of the triangle for single beats, then roll the metal striker around the inside for continuous sound. Have volunteers then play with the recording, using **Listening Map #11** as their guide.

CLOSURE:

Have the students remember that the **"The Toreador Song"** is sung as a baritone solo in the opera, **"Carmen,"** by the bullfighter character, **Escamillo**. He tells the admiring crowd about the dangers and glories of his exciting profession. Recall what happens to Escamillo, Carmen and Don José at the end of the opera.

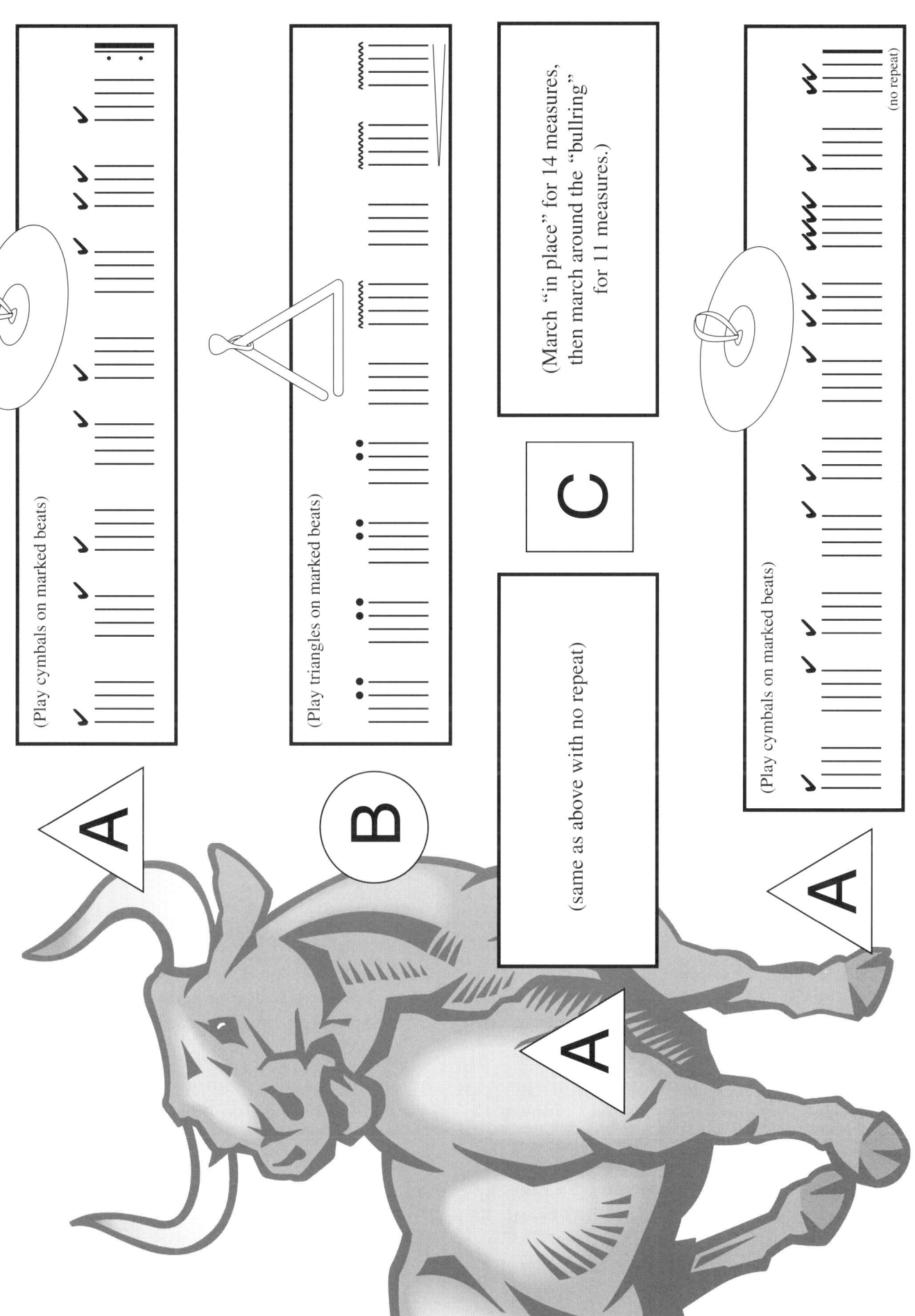

LISTENING TO THE MUSIC OF BIZET

SELECTION: *"Farandole from L'Arlesienne Suite No. 2"*
(CD track #12)
COMPOSER: Georges Bizet
TIME: 3:26

BACKGROUND:
1. The last of four movements in this suite **(pastorale, intermezzo, minuet and farandole)** begins with a strong march motif (**A section**), followed by a lively dance played by the flutes (**B section**). Both themes are played alternately and then together in the final section for a robust ending.
2. The ***farandole*** is a popular folk dance in France and Spain, being indicative of Bizet's work, who as a French composer worked Spanish color into many of his works. The melody from an old French Christmas Carol, *"The March of the Three Kings,"* is used prominently in this piece during the **A sections**.

PREPARATION:
1. Notice when the **A section** is first repeated, it is done as a 'round' where the theme is pronounced by higher strings, then echoed almost exactly by lower strings.
2. Listen as a single tambourine introduces the dance (**B section**) the first time it is heard. Keep listening as the tambourine continues to play steady accented eighth notes throughout the piece.
3. You will hear an effect called a **'glissando'** (a flowing, unaccented upsweep of fast notes) performed by the strings for unique emphasis in **B section** variations.

INVOLVEMENT:
1. Using **Listening Map #12** as their guide, have students follow the **dots** that represent actual beats and the **arrows** that direct the listener's attention from one section to the next in sequence.
2. Have the students raise their hands when they hear the majestic **A section theme** repeated as a round performed by the strings. Select a 'round' the class knows well and sing it in two groups to get the full effect of what is happening in the orchestra at this point.
3. Choose a familiar 'partner' song (two distinct tunes) and sing it in two groups, which represents the final section of this piece when **A and B** are effectively played at the same time.
4. Practice tapping steady eighth notes at a fast tempo, slightly accenting the first tap of each measure. Next, transfer this technique to a tambourine, playing lightly in a folk dance mood. Have a capable volunteer play along with the recording, using a tap-shake technique.

CLOSURE:
Divide the class into two groups, having one group stand each time the **A section** theme is heard and the other side stand on the **B section** theme. Decide what will happen at the end of the piece.

Listening Map #12

"Farandole from L'Arlesienne Suite No. 2"
Georges Bizet

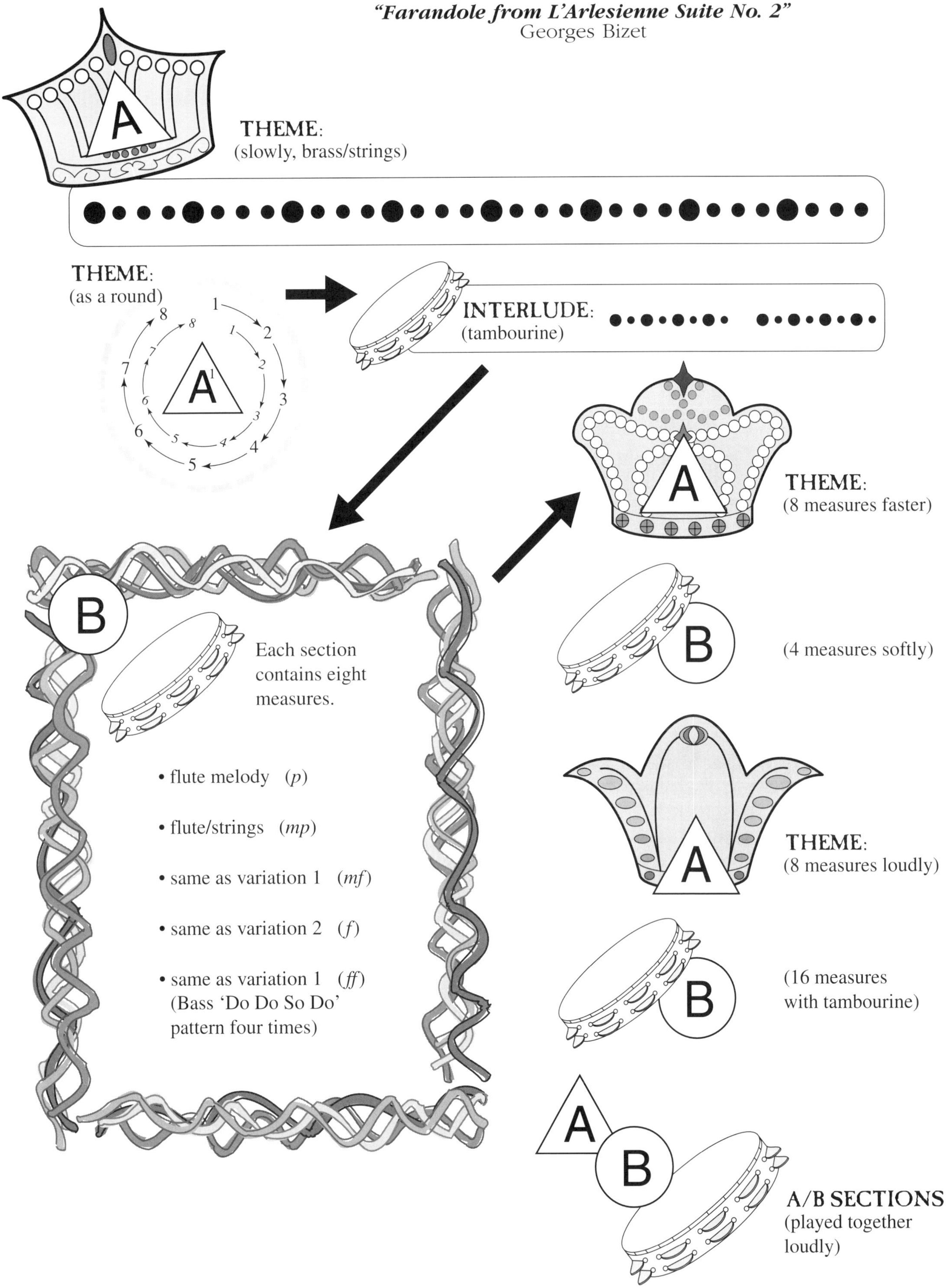

THEME: (slowly, brass/strings)

THEME: (as a round)

INTERLUDE: (tambourine)

THEME: (8 measures faster)

B — Each section contains eight measures.
- flute melody (*p*)
- flute/strings (*mp*)
- same as variation 1 (*mf*)
- same as variation 2 (*f*)
- same as variation 1 (*ff*) (Bass 'Do Do So Do' pattern four times)

B (4 measures softly)

THEME: (8 measures loudly)

B (16 measures with tambourine)

A/B SECTIONS (played together loudly)

Permission to photocopy the above activity, limited to one school only.

BIBLIOGRAPHY

All About Music, by Frederic Fay Swift and Willare Musser, Belwin Inc., Rockville, New York, 1960.

Classical Music, Robert Ainsley, General Editor, Smithmark Publishers, 16 East 32nd Street, New York, 1995.

Classical Music, the 50 Greatest Composers and Their 1,000 Greatest Works by Phil Goulding, Fawcett Columbine, New York, 1992.

The Dictionary of Composers, edited by Charles Osbourne, A Crescendo Book, Taplinger Publishing Company, New York, 1977.

The Dictionary of Composers, A Listening Companion, by Eric Glider, Wing Books, New York, 1993.

Encyclopedia of the Great Composers and Their Music, by Milton Cross, Volumes I and II, Doubleday and Company, New York, 1962.

Franz Liszt, The Man and His Music, Alan Walker, Editor, Taplinger Publisher, New York, 1970.

Great Composers, edited by Marshall Cavendish, Chartwell Books, Inc., 110 Enterprise Avenue, New Jersey, 1989.

Great Composers and Their Music (The), by Janet Klevberg, Hal Leonard Corporation, 1994.

Guiness Book of Music (The), by Robert and Celia Dearling with Brian Rust, Guiness Superlatives Limited, 2 Cecil Court, London Road, Enfield, Middlesex, 1976, 1981 and 1986.

Handel's Messiah, A Celebration, by Richard Luckett, A Helen and Kurt Wolff Book, Harcourt Brace and Company, New York, 1992.

International Library of Music (The), The University Society, Inc., Educational Publishers, New York, 1966.

Involvement with Music, by DeLone and Winold Christ, Harper's College Press, New York, 1975.

Keyboard Jr. and Young Keyboard Jr., The Magazine for Music Appreciation, School Edition, Ian Mininberg, Editor, 1346 Chapel Street, New Haven, Connecticut.

Lives of the Great Composers (The), by Harold Schonberg, W. W. Morton and Co., Inc. New York, 1970.

Music Guide, an Introduction, by Stanley Sadie and Alison Latham, Prentice-Hall, Inc., Englewood Cliffs, New Jersey, 1986.

Music of Man (The), by Yehudi Menuhin and Curtis W. Davis, Methuen, Inc., 733 Third Avenue, New York, 1979.

Skeletons from the Opera Closet, by David Groover and C. C. Conner, St. Martin's Press, New York, 1986.

Treasury of Grand Opera (A), Henry W. Simon, Simon and Schuster, New York, 1965.

Vintage Guide to Classical Music (The), Jan Swafford, Vintage Books, Random House, New York, 1992.

What We Hear in Music, by Anne Shaw Faulkner, Educational Department, RCA Victor Division, Camden, New Jersey, 1943.

Wonderful World of Dance (The), by Arnold Haskell, Doubleday and Company, Garden City, New York, 1969.

ABOUT THE AUTHOR

Betsy Henderson is the Elementary Fine Arts Coordinator for the Garland Independent School District in Garland, Texas, as well as an elementary assistant principal. An author of the music textbook series, Share the Music, published by Macmillan/McGraw-Hill Publishing Company, Mrs. Henderson has served as guest clinician for over one hundred workshops and choir festivals in educational and church settings.

Mrs. Henderson has served as the Elementary State Chairperson for both the Texas Music Educators Association and the Texas Choral Directors Association. She is also the Coordinator of Children's Music Ministry at First United Methodist Church in Garland, TX, were she supervises five graded choirs and directs the 5th/6th grade choir with an upper grade Orff instrumental group. Mrs. Henderson has directed the award-winning Garland All-City Girls Choir for over twenty years.

THE COMPOSERS' SPECIALS

FROM THE DEVINE ENTERTAINMENT VIDEO SERIES

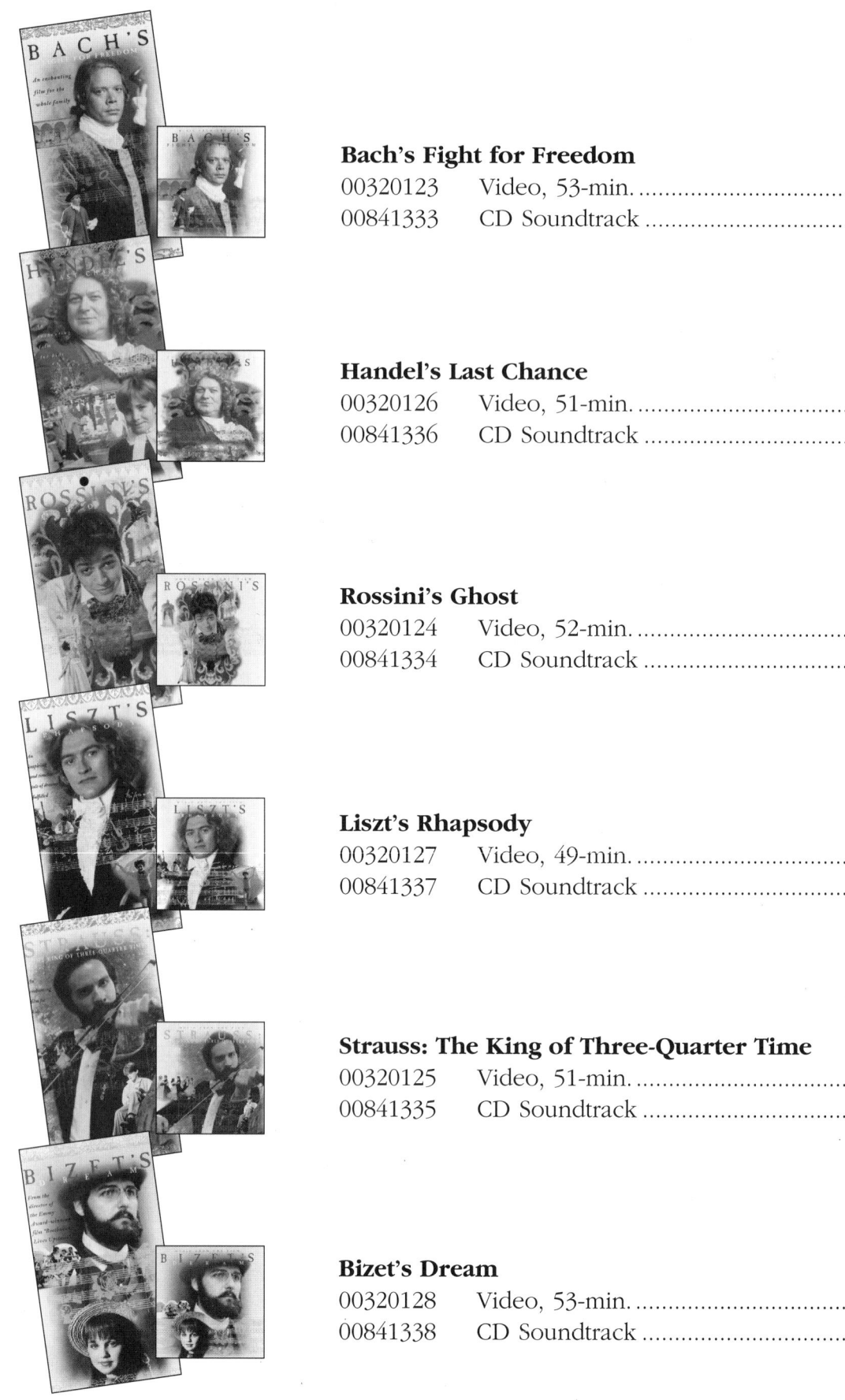

Bach's Fight for Freedom
00320123   Video, 53-min. $19.95
00841333   CD Soundtrack $12.95

Handel's Last Chance
00320126   Video, 51-min. $19.95
00841336   CD Soundtrack $12.95

Rossini's Ghost
00320124   Video, 52-min. $19.95
00841334   CD Soundtrack $12.95

Liszt's Rhapsody
00320127   Video, 49-min. $19.95
00841337   CD Soundtrack $12.95

Strauss: The King of Three-Quarter Time
00320125   Video, 51-min. $19.95
00841335   CD Soundtrack $12.95

Bizet's Dream
00320128   Video, 53-min. $19.95
00841338   CD Soundtrack $12.95